I0617905

YOUR GREATEST LIFE SERIES

DROP YOUR SWORD

Letting God Fight Your Battles

You will not need to fight in this battle. Position yourselves,
stand still, and see the salvation of the LORD, who is with you.
—II Chronicles 20:17

MARION GRACE

Siretona
CREATIVE

Published by Siretona Creative. www.siretona.com

978-1-988983-87-5 Electronic book
978-1-988983-86-8 Paperback

Cover and interior design by Travis Williams

Cover art:
Sunrise photo licensed from iStock/VR_Studio
Model with sword provided by Candace Moore Photography
Title and cover text typeset in Palatino

Interior layout:
Text typeset in Minion Pro
Section, chapter, and running heads typeset in Trajan Pro 3

Distributed to the trade by Ingram Book Company.

For they did not gain possession of the land
by their own sword,
Nor did their own arm save them;
But it was Your right hand—
Your arm, and the light of Your countenance,
Because You favored them.
—Psalm 44:3

To my Lord and Savior who is
the one that has caused me to stand.
All I do is unto you and for you.

To my brothers and sisters in Christ
who know, or suspect, that there is more
than the status quo and merely surviving each
day. I pray these pages will help you soar with
the eagles and live a victorious life
of joy and freedom.

CONTENTS

FOREWORD

Marion Grace is a strong warrior in the Kingdom of God. I was introduced to her through mutual friends (who happened to be her pastors) during my own battle with bone marrow cancer. Since she had already gone through it with wonderful victory, she was a beacon to me through her prayers and encouragement during my journey to recovery and healing. Her first book, *Your Greatest Life: Overcoming Depression, Divorce, and Critical Illness*, along with her testimony helped me greatly. The Bible tells us in Revelation 19:10 that the testimony of Jesus is the Spirit of prophecy and I received this as my outcome.

Her second book, *Drop Your Sword: Letting God Fight your Battles*, is a word you must have in your repertoire. She has a grasp of God's principles on how to live in this world by trusting and allowing God to be in charge. With this tool, you will be more firmly established in His Word and experience victory in your life in whatever area you are struggling. God is good and He is good all the time.

VALERIE MICHAUD BENNETT
Memphis, Tennessee
Women's Pastor Emeritus,
former co-host on the Miracle Channel,
Pastor at Large

INTRODUCTION

While writing the first book in this series, *Your Greatest Life*, I had a defining "a-ha" moment of inspiration from God about fighting my battles. This epiphany came to me when I finished and was trying to get feedback and constructive criticism. Not one person I asked would even read it and the editing process seemed to take forever. What started as such excitement and enthusiasm in doing something for God turned into discouragement and deflation just because of circumstances. Sound familiar?

When something does not go as we think it should, what is the first thing we believe? I will make the first confession that I thought it was an attack of the enemy. That devil was trying to stop my book from being published. Well, I am sure he did not like the fact that a book helping people resist him was being distributed, but I learned a very important lesson about recognizing what is and what is not an attack from the enemy. The enemy would like to make you think that he is all big and powerful and always able to mess you up, but that is not the reality. He is not that big of a deal. When I calmed down and talked to God about this, He reminded me of Gideon and his mere three hundred men going out to fight an entire army (Judges 7).

When people's plans don't get in God's way and we don't try to help Him out, God gets all the glory. Perhaps I was not supposed to get a lot of opinions and input so that God would get all the glory for this series. We need to learn that there are differences in attacks of the enemy. Some are outright stealing, killing, and destroying attempts, but others can be a setup for a disguised God-opportunity. Other situations may look like an attack but may be a guiding circumstance or a directional moment.

In this book I want to share with you how to examine circumstances in the light of God's Word, and how to respond in a way that will bring you swift and sure victory, not beating the air and letting the enemy run you around in circles. Victory is not always in the absence of a challenge, but in its powerlessness to affect you. We win when we operate above it and know who we are—when we learn how to stand still in the knowledge that Jesus has already won for us. God gives us clear instructions about recognizing the enemy in John 10:10. The thief does not come except to steal and to kill and to destroy. These criteria will help us identify the situation ninety-nine percent of the time.

Believe me, when I was lying in a hospital bed, diagnosed with final-stage bone marrow cancer, as well as enduring unbearable emotional pain, I knew the identity of the battle. There was no mystery as to the stealing, killing, and destroying characteristics of this situation. There are many levels of attacks from life and death, like mine was, to financial hardships, serious relationship struggles, people coming against you, and thought-life challenges, just to name a few. This is common to all of us.

Many Christians are facing mountains that they desperately want, and need, to be moved. (Let's be honest—mountain ranges, right?) We lift our eyes to God and cry out in self-pity, "Why God, why?" I know this so well—I have been there many times. I believe most of us have faith and our hearts are sincere before the Lord, but the problem is that we are wielding the wrong sword, beating the air, and tiring ourselves out. The world says to fight for your rights and make sure you are looking after your own interests. I am sure we are all familiar with and have used the phrase, "What about me? What about me!"

The thing is, in God's economy there is little room for self-focus. When it's just *woe is me; me, me, me,* you will not get far. In the Bible, the only sword we are told to fight with is the sword of the Spirit, the Word of God. God's ways are always opposite the world's and will never seem to make sense or pamper our flesh and self. My friends, lay down your fleshly, heavy, war-torn sword, and walk with me as I cast some light through experience and success on God's amazing plan for winning your battles. This is a book for those who have always suspected that there is more to this Christian life than just enduring trials with "humility" for Jesus. It is for those who, like me, would rather smash through them in a blaze of glory, triumph, and joy while leaving them in the dust. Mine is a perspective that trials are an empowerment opportunity; the joy of the end result overshadowing any temporary pain.

You, my friend, have a power position that will send the devil running for cover in utter frustration and leave you laughing hilariously. Let's begin.

SECTION 1

A Man After God's Own Heart: Lessons From David

He raised up unto them David to be their king;
to whom also he gave their testimony, and said,
I have found David the son of Jesse, a man after
mine own heart, which shall fulfill all my will.
—Acts 13:22, KJV

SECTION 1

A Man After God's Own Heart: Lessons From David

CHAPTER 1

The Secret Weapon of Praise

> Yet I know that you are most holy; it's indisputable.
> You are God-Enthroned, surrounded with songs,
> living among the shouts of praise of your princely
> people. —Psalm 22:3, TPT

I AM BEGINNING THIS BOOK ON THE SUBJECT OF PRAISE AND worship for two very important reasons: who it attracts and who it repels. The fact that God inhabits the praises of His people is a fundamental truth in Christianity. When you need to be in God's presence, begin to worship Him. This is how I begin each day, because I know how much I need to be near Him. This is especially true if there is any trouble in my life. (Did I say "if"?)

We enter into His gates with thanksgiving and praise (Psalm 100:4). Praise and worship are a significant part of our communion with God—our relationship with God. Think about Psalm 22:3 He lives among our praises. When we are in trouble, we first need to know that God is with us.

Hebrews 13:5 is another fundamental truth and can surely be depended on: "For He Himself has said, 'I will never leave you nor forsake you.'" Can I risk being honest here and confess that I do not always feel His presence? I am sure we have all been there. Do you know that you do not have to stay there? When I find myself in that situation, I do what I learned to do when I was lying in the hospital with cancer: I press play. When I begin to worship God out of a sincere heart He ALWAYS shows up. His Word says so.

I was reading a book by a popular Christian author and was loving it until I read one thing that greatly disturbed me. They said that God will test your loyalty and your devotion to Him by sometimes being silent and not allowing you to feel His presence within you; that this was God's way of causing you to become more mature and we all will face this from time to time on purpose.

They referenced two Old Testament examples: one of David speaking in the Psalms when he was discouraged (as in Psalm 13:1-2) and a discouraging moment in the testing of Job (chapter 23). This teaching jarred my spirit and almost made me feel sick. I immediately went to God about it and will share with you what God taught me in case anyone tries to convince you of this very common, but very wrong idea.

First, let's explore the Hebrew word in the Old Testament that is used to try and back up this idea. When you understand what the words used in the Bible mean, you will be set free, and no one can take it away from you. This word *hide* here is "sawthar" (*Strong's*, Hebrew #5641). When I looked up the meaning, I discovered that there are five words, all with the same root. The root seems to have different applications depending on the context. The basic definition includes to keep secret, keep hidden, to hide by covering, to keep close, conceal, to cover up in a good or bad way (wherever *Strong's* uses the negative absent or demolish, it prefaces with "figuratively"), protection, and to secretly place. I am sure that if you are a Word person at all, your mind is going to many scriptures where God talks of hiding us. Let me remind you of a few:

> Keep me as the apple of Your eye; Hide me under
> the shadow of Your wings (Psalm 17:8).

> For in the time of trouble He shall hide me in His
> pavilion; In the secret place of His tabernacle He
> shall hide me; He shall set me high upon a rock
> (Psalm 27:5).

> You shall hide them in the secret place of Your
> presence from the plots of man;

> You shall keep them secretly in a pavilion from
> the strife of tongues (Psalm 31:20).

> Hide me from the secret plots of the wicked, from
> the rebellion of the workers of iniquity (Psalm 64:2).

There are some instances where this word is used in a different context, like in Isaiah 45:15, but please note the context is talking about God's enemies. I also want to comment that when David was crying out to God while feeling that God was hiding from him, it may have been only that—a feeling. Although there are many instances where David's crying out to God in this manner is accurately recorded, it is important to see what he wrote in Psalm 31:22 (TPT):

> I spoke hastily when I said, "The Lord has
> deserted me."
> For in truth, you did hear my prayer and came to
> rescue me.

We cannot build a doctrine on the accurate record of how a man was crying out to God during a bad day unless it agrees with solid teaching from God's Word. This is also the man who cried out, "Kill them all, God." David was a man after God's own heart, but he was human and living under the Old Covenant. I am very glad it is recorded because I can relate without feeling condemned. If the man after God's heart can have bad days, then I will too.

Since Jesus died and rose from the dead, we now are living in the New Covenant with God the Father. One of the best parts of that New Covenant is that we have the Holy Spirit living inside us as a seal and a guarantee that we are God's purchased possession; we are His children.

> Now He who establishes us with you in Christ
> and has anointed us is God, who also has sealed
> us and given us the Spirit in our hearts as a
> guarantee (II Corinthians 1:21-22).

The saints in the Old Testament did not have this privilege. As anointed and as godly as some of them were, they did not have the Holy Spirit living inside them; they had the Holy Spirit "upon" them at certain times. There is a huge difference and that is the reason Jesus says in Matthew 11:11, "There has not risen one greater than John the Baptist; but he who is least in the kingdom of heaven is greater than he."

I want you to read that passage in several translations right now, because it will set you free.[1] YOU, my friend, are being called one greater than John the Baptist. YOU have the Holy Spirit living inside you so naturally, His presence is always with you. You have the opportunity to have communion with God on a level no one in the Old Testament ever did, not even David. The Holy Spirit was sent to be our helper and comforter in every way. I know this may be a hard concept to grasp, but it's not me saying so, it is God. God is not going to shut down His Spirit in you to test you. How could He? Then He would cease to be the guarantee and the seal. Look at this beautiful passage:

> And I will pray the Father, and He will give you
> another Helper, that He may abide with you
> forever (John 14:16).

Do you see the words "abide with you forever"? Do I need to remind you that God is not a man that He should lie? We do not even have to look at this in the Greek or Aramaic dictionary because it means the same in English. The word translated "helper" is *comforter* ("parakletos," *Strong's* #3875) and means "intercessor, consoler, and advocate." The very definition implies that He will be with us in our hour of greatest need. When Jesus died and paid the price for our sins, the Bible says the veil in the temple was torn from top to bottom by God. That means we now have access. That means now we can come boldly before the throne of God. We are now sons, not servants. These things were unheard of up till that time. God wanted His children to have a whole new relationship with Him and to be inseparable from Him.

> He who has My commandments and keeps them,
> it is he who loves Me. And he who loves Me will
> be loved by My Father, and I will love him and
> manifest Myself to him (John 14:21).

> Draw near to God and He will draw near to you
> (James 4:8).

> Let us, therefore, come boldly to the throne of
> grace, that we may obtain mercy and find grace to
> help in time of need (Hebrews 4:16).

> Therefore, brethren, having boldness to enter the
> Holiest by the blood of Jesus, by a new and living
> way which He consecrated for us, through the veil,
> that is, His flesh (Hebrews 10:19).

In reading any of these verses do you see anything about approaching Him and receiving silence? No. This is His new way, His New Covenant. There is no such thing as, "Let's see how you do on your own." If there is, then what is the point? The Bible calls our own efforts "filthy rags" in Isaiah 64:6. Jesus paid too high a price for you to ever leave you on your own. God often describes His relationship with us as a sheep/shepherd or a father/child picture. A good shepherd would never leave a sheep to get through trouble on its own. Rather, he would pick it up and carry it out. As parents, would we ever just refuse to be there for our kids if they came to us and asked? I know I wouldn't, and I do not think any would. Should we accuse God of this? I would never believe it. That is not the God I have come to know. I have already admitted that I do not always feel His presence, but when I honestly look at it, it is always, always, my doing.

Let me give you an example. An older married couple was driving to a dinner date and the wife was thinking about times past when they were younger and more romantic. She turned to her husband and asked, "Remember when we used to sit close in the car, and you always put your arm around me. Why don't we do that anymore?" The husband looked at her and said, "I haven't moved." This may not be a perfect example, but it makes the point. If there is a problem, we are the ones who moved out of position. He never moves away from us.

Let me give you another picture that may help you understand from another angle. Do you always feel loving and close to your spouse? Probably not. Does this mean your spouse is no longer there, along with all the attributes of the marriage? Is your marriage covenant no longer real? No, of course not. Sometimes there are situations in my marriage that cause friction, hurt, or upset, and I do not feel the way I want to. Despite that fact, if my husband was in need, I would be there in a heartbeat, and vice versa. My ruffled feathers do not remove my action of love; my unconditional commitment of love. Neither do the feelings remove my husband's love, even though he knows I am in a bad place. To me, it shows another aspect of our relationship with God.

I am hitting this teaching hard right at the beginning because I believe that without this understanding, we will have trouble believing all of the seemingly outrageous promises God makes to us in His Word. If we do not know how much He loves us and that His presence is always with us, how could we believe Ephesians 3:20, which tells us He will do exceedingly above all we can ask or think?[2] How could we believe that God will give us His very own kind of life as in Romans 8:11?[3] How could we possibly believe that God will give us the very desires of our hearts as stated in Psalm 37:4?[4] Most outrageous of all, how could we believe that by Jesus' stripes we have already been provided with healing for our bodies (I Peter 2:24)?[5] Without knowing the extravagant, passionate, unending love that God has for us we would not be able to believe it. We might think, like traditional "religion" teaches, that we deserved the trouble; that God might be teaching us a lesson.

I know when these "dry times" or "wilderness experiences" come, it is usually when I am going through severe trials. I expect that it is the same for most of us. Why would God be silent just when you need Him the most? That is not the character of the God I have come to know. It is inconsistent with what I see in His Word. Can I share with you what I have learned and observed? It is not in any way meant to be condemning, but an outside-the-box perspective that may help you avoid this.

Instead of saying that it must be God that has pulled away from us, could it be possible that we have allowed the trial to put us in a position or mindset that God cannot engage with? Let me explain. When I was facing stage four cancer and was being bombarded by every negative report imaginable, I could have responded in several ways. What if I had entertained fear? What if I had remained silent in my confession and began to listen to the enemy? What if I had allowed doubt or unbelief to creep in? All of these are the opposite of faith and can quench the fellowship of God in our lives. God cannot engage actively with a person holding these non-faith attitudes. He is a faithful God and responds to faith.

> But without faith it is impossible to please Him,
> for he who comes to God must believe that He is,
> and that He is a rewarder of those who diligently
> seek Him (Hebrews 11:6).

Based on what I see in God's Word, this is what I suspect is happening in these dry times. Let me encourage you again in saying you do not need to stay there.

When we recognize the problem, we can begin to take steps to get back in His presence, to pull down the barrier that we had allowed to form. Begin to worship Him. As He inhabits our worship—trust me—the fear, the doubt, or whatever is nagging at us, will flee (James 4:7) and you will be back where you are supposed to be. We, as God's children, are made for abiding in Him.

> Abide in Me, and I in you. As the branch cannot
> bear fruit of itself, unless it abides in the vine,
> neither can you, unless you abide in Me (John 15:4).

The word *abide* means, "To stay in a given place or state, to continue, dwell, endure, remain, be present and stand with" ("meno," *Strong's* #3306). This sounds very permanent to me. We are born again for abiding, relationship, and fellowship with God the Father through Jesus Christ His Son. I have found that the first step is always praise and worship. When I am facing a problem, if I am feeling discouraged, if I am hurt, angry, or feeling ill, I have learned to immediately press play. Worship is the quickest way into His presence. In the next few pages, we will look at the various aspects of this very powerful gift that God has provided for us to live triumphant, peaceful, and complete Christian lives.

Singing and Shouting

At the beginning of this chapter, I mentioned two important aspects of praise and worship: who it attracts and who it repels. If you have read my first book in this series, *Your Greatest Life: Overcoming Depression, Divorce, and Critical Illness,* you will remember that I like to aggravate the devil, because he tried relentlessly to destroy my life for so long. I understand that the only essential part is the closeness to God, but I would be lying if I did not admit that I like to drive the devil nuts now that I am wise to his tactics. I take some pleasure in threatening him, whenever he comes around to try and bother me, with the fact that it will result in my singing at the top of my lungs about the blood of Jesus. Trust me, he will leave. He hates hearing it. That may sound funny, but it is as serious as can be. Praise is a weapon.

God's high and holy praises fill their mouths, for
their shouted praises are their weapons of war!

These warring weapons will bring vengeance on
every opposing force and every resistant power—to
bind kings with chains and rulers with iron shackles.
Praise-filled warriors will enforce the judgment-
doom decreed against their enemies. This is the
glorious honor he gives to all his godly lovers.
Hallelujah! Praise the Lord! (Psalm 149:6-9, TPT)

You have taught children and babies to sing
praises to you because of your enemies. And so
you silence your enemies and destroy those who
try to get even (Psalm 8:2, NCV).

Why are praise and worship so powerful? It is because of what
it does in the spirit realm. We have already seen that God inhabits
the praises of His people so we know it brings God's power
immediately to the scene, but it also sends out those spiritual
vibrations into the atmosphere that the enemy cannot resist.

Let me remind you of my teaching from my first book about
the seven sons of Sceva in Acts 19:13-15.

Then some of the itinerant Jewish exorcists took
it upon themselves to call the name of the Lord
Jesus over those who had evil spirits, saying, "We
exorcise you by the Jesus whom Paul preaches."
Also, there were seven sons of Sceva, a Jewish
chief priest, who did so. And the evil spirit
answered and said, "Jesus I know, and Paul I
know; but who are you?"

Here we see men who do not have the Spirit of God trying to take authority over evil spirits. Note the spirits' answer very carefully. They knew Jesus and Paul. I looked up this word, *known*, in *Strong's Concordance* (#1987, #2168, and #3563), and found that it means "to comprehend fully and know your standing." Very interesting, isn't it, that these evil spirits, who hated Jesus and Paul as their enemy, admitted that they knew their place before them. I believe it was the spiritual vibrations that came out of them that the spirits saw and were afraid of. They saw the strength of their faith and authority through the vibrations it caused in the spirit realm. Look at this verse:

> For we do not wrestle against flesh and blood, but
> against principalities, against powers, against the
> rulers of the darkness of this age, against spiritual
> hosts of wickedness in the heavenly places
> (Ephesians 6:12).

The word *wrestle* here is the key. It literally means "to vibrate against violently" ("pale" and "ballo," *Strong's* #3823 and #906). This is where so many Christians get in trouble because they think they have to wrestle with the devil, as we commonly know that word, when in reality all we have to do is bombard him with our praise vibrations. That's why praise is a weapon. In the Old Testament, we see several examples of God instructing His armies to send the praisers first. Here are my favorites:

> Now when they began to sing and to praise,
> the Lord set ambushes against the people

of Ammon, Moab, and Mount Seir, who had come against Judah; and they were defeated (II Chronicles 20:22).

Then the men of Judah gave a shout; and as the men of Judah shouted, it happened that God struck Jeroboam and all Israel before Abijah and Judah (II Chronicles 13:15).

So the people shouted when the priests blew the trumpets. And it happened when the people heard the sound of the trumpet, and the people shouted with a great shout, that the wall fell down flat. Then the people went up into the city, every man straight before him, and they took the city (Joshua 6:20).

Then the children of Israel arose and went up to the house of God to inquire of God. They said, "Which of us shall go up first to battle against the children of Benjamin?" The Lord said, "Judah first!" (Judges 20:18).

This last verse is significant because of the phrase, "Judah first." The name *Judah* is the Hebrew word *Yadah*, which means praise. It is no accident that King David, the greatest worshiper of all time, descended from this tribe. God is saying to always praise first. It will put you in a power position.

Dancing and Twirling

Another very important and effective part of praise and worship is the physical participation and demonstration of our bodies before the Lord. I know a lot of reserved and religious people are not very comfortable with this concept, but it is so prevalent in scripture that we should not and cannot ignore it. Remember, anything God instructs us to do in His Word is always for our benefit. Keep an open mind as we explore this teaching. I will only refer to the verses that directly address dancing before the Lord because there are too many in which God instructs his people to dance and rejoice in general.

> Then David danced before the Lord with all his might, and David was wearing a linen ephod (2 Samuel 6:14).

> When the Chest of the Covenant of God entered the City of David, Michal, Saul's daughter, was watching from a window. When she saw King David dancing ecstatically, she was filled with contempt (I Chronicles 15:29, MSG).

> Let them praise His name with dancing; Let them sing praises to Him with timbrels and a harp (Psalm 149:3, NLV).

> Praise Him with the timbrel and dance; Praise Him with stringed instruments and flutes! (Psalm 150:4).

> Then he broke through and transformed all my
> wailing into a whirling dance of ecstatic praise!
> (Psalm 30:11, TPT).

I would like to share with you the various definitions of the word dance as it is interpreted in our English Bible. You may be surprised. According to *Strong's Concordance*, "machowl" (Hebrew #4234) and "chiyl" (#2342) mean to twirl and twist in a fashion that might look like someone writhing in pain. "Raqad"—I love this one—means to stomp, to spring about wildly for joy, to jump, leap and skip *(Strong's #7540)*. It certainly sounds like it is to be more than tapping your foot. This sounds like some serious bodily rejoicing. If you look at the scriptures above in Psalms 149 and 150 it clearly says, "Let them." That sounds like God is telling us to do something. Don't shout me down while I'm preaching good now.

Perhaps there is a reason God wants us to do this. I think we can find part of the answer in David's response to his wife recorded in II Samuel 6:22. He answers, "And I will be even more undignified than this, and will be humble in my own sight." I think this sort of demonstration shows a sense of abandonment before God. It is something we do to show we are not self-conscious, but rather God-conscious. We are worshiping God and we do not care what we look like to anyone else except God. It is a form of surrender of our human pride, our submission to Him. This pleases God.

As I have mentioned before, there is little room for selfishness in our relationship with God. If I said that this type of activity could be described as a form of crucifying our flesh (Galatians 5:24), I think it would carry merit. If we are indeed crucified with

Christ and are no longer living for ourselves, then I do wonder why we make excuses to not do some of the things scripture tells us to do. Just saying. Besides the more important spiritual reasons, there are also physical and psychological benefits to all forms of praise and worship.

Anything God tells us to do in His Word is so multi-faceted and deep that we could never fully grasp it all, but I will share with you what I have learned and encourage you to do a little digging for yourself. I saw the effects of praise and worship on my mental and physical health before I ever really began to understand it. During my time in the hospital and the several years of battling for my life following the initial diagnosis, I spent a lot of time with God. I was extremely weak and for a lot of the time, all I could do was press play on my tablet and worship Him while soaking in His presence. That was all I had at that time. Little did I know that it was the most powerful thing working for me and the reason my body and mind were miraculously recovering.

As I became stronger, I would praise and dance in my living room because it always made me feel better. I would always go up to the alter in church services during praise and worship time to participate because I did not care what people thought. I am very uncoordinated, even my kids laugh at my awkwardness, but the benefits are worth it. Pay close attention to this because the gift of praise and worship is a level playing field. Anyone can participate, it costs nothing, and no one can take it away from you.

In my research, I came across the study "Neurophysiological Benefits of Worship" by Michael Liedke, DNP. In it, he reports such robust and undeniable results that one must recognize the credibility and accuracy. Could there ever be any doubt? After all, it is God's idea. I am not a scientist, so I will explain it best I can. According to this study, worship increases the volume and activity of the brain's cingulate cortex, which controls empathetic thinking and feeling and the ability to forgive. Worship also registered a hypoactivation (down-regulation) of the amygdala cells in the base of the brain, where strong and often negative emotions and responses are controlled. So, let's keep this simple, take these two facts only, and tie them in with Jesus' teachings. If our empathetic thinking and feelings are increased, we can forgive, care about, and love other people more. Loving one another is the whole idea, not to mention the only command of the New Covenant in Jesus. In layperson's terms, we will become more kind and loving people. Now let's look at the effect of the hypo-activated responses.

Those who worshiped regularly showed a significant reduction in the intense responses of depression, anxiety, PTSD, and pain, to name a few. I am not surprised; I have proven it in my situation. Because of the reduction in these strong responses that are toxic to the body, there was also a significant lowering of high blood pressure, high blood sugar, and inflammation. Does this sound like a great deal to anyone else? I am not telling anyone to go off their medication, but I will repeat what I said in my first book: "Have everything working for you" (p. 22). God works well with medicine. Put God's super on the natural.

I will also recommend the 21-Day Brain Detox program by Dr. Caroline Leaf, which practically expands on these concepts. I loved the program as it taught very clearly the importance and power of what you put your thoughts toward and how it affects you in all areas.

Meditating

This is the part of worship we often associate with quietness or the stance of "just being" with God. The posture is sometimes described in scripture as kneeling or bowing in reverence. This is the part of worship embodied in the scripture, "Be still, and know that I am God" (Psalm 46:10).

When I look at my own life, these are the moments when I am just sitting or lying down and soaking in His presence as soft, peaceful worship music plays, or I am just thinking about all the wonders of God. These are often the quiet moments when I listen for His voice, and He speaks to me. Before I ever sit down to write anything, I always make sure I take the time to practice this type of worship because I only want to write what God wants. I only want to say what He says. I have tried to write without doing this, but it never works; there is no anointing and I end up wasting my time. David spoke of this form of worship often:

> When I remember You on my bed, I meditate on You in the night watches (Psalm 63:6).

> Meditate within your heart on your bed, and be still (Psalm 4:4).

> I will meditate on the glorious splendor of Your majesty, and on Your wondrous works. (Psalm 145:5).

> Oh come, let us worship and bow down; Let us kneel before the Lord our Maker (Psalm 95:6).

This meditation also includes thinking about His Word, which is also worship. Anything we do to acknowledge, exalt, give place to, or sacrifice for God is worship. He loves our worship because it is our heart. He loves for us to seek after Him in every way because of the relationship and because He knows what it will do for us. He knows that our entire beings, which are in His image, are made to respond to and fully function in His presence.

You get to a certain "full" level when you know you have been in God's presence. You know what I mean—you feel light, happy, and content. I am sure you also know, as I do, when your levels are low. For me, I recognize it by the sense of agitation, being unsettled, and generally blue. I know immediately to go fill my tank with His presence. We are not designed to live outside of Him. We are not meant to do anything God asks us to do in His Word with our own strength.

Can I go off on a little bunny trail here? I think someone needs to hear this. I am sure, like me, you have read devotionals and heard sermons encouraging you to watch your temper, watch your mouth, walk in love, just decide to be happy, and take control of your flesh. All excellent and biblically based things, right? My problem with these teachings is that they can be presented as a list of dos and don'ts. If you were a "good" Christian, you would do these things. Failure to be able to control these fleshly things is the reason a lot of Christians get condemned and discouraged.

Listen to me very carefully. You were NEVER meant to do any of this on your own. The Holy Spirit within you gives you the power to change. It is all God's ability and none of your own. When I mess up, I realize that I have not spent enough time with God, and I just get to it. I have no self-righteous expectations of myself because I know what I am without Him. I want to please God and be like Jesus, so I do not struggle, grit my teeth, try harder, or beat myself up; I just run to the source. He is the only one who can change me, so I let him do it. Please pause and let these words minister to you right now.

As we have seen above, praise and worship are powerful weapons for the battles outside and those within us. When I am facing hardship, a difficult decision, bad news, turmoil, a personal attack, pressure, fear, or illness, my immediate go-to is worship in His presence—and His peace and comfort never fail me.

When I draw near to God, He always draws near to me (James 4:8), and He will draw near to you as well. The type of worship depends on the particular circumstance. If it is an outside attack trying to steal something from me, it demands shouting. If it is inner turmoil or fear, I get quiet before the Lord and meditate on Him with soft worship music. If faced with confusion or a difficult decision, I will go to His Word for the answer. All of this is worship. You will find, with practice, what will work for you in your circumstance. God's Word tells us to be in this mindset continually, to have a daily lifestyle of prayer and praise. I now understand why I was able to handle and get through everything that happened to me. I certainly did wonder for a while how I did. Not that my thinking was correct all the time, but I am very aware now of the fact that what was designed to destroy me twice over could not. It could not break through the presence of God in my life. Every single aspect of our faithful and loving God is amazing.

> Therefore by Him, let us continually offer the sacrifice of praise to God, that is, the fruit of our lips, giving thanks to His name (Hebrews 13:15).

Continue earnestly in prayer, being vigilant in it
with thanksgiving (Colossians 4:2).

You will keep him in perfect peace, whose
mind is stayed on You, because he trusts in You
(Isaiah 26:3).

I want to end this chapter focusing on this last verse because it
speaks of our staying in peace. According to *Strong's Concordance,*
the word *stayed* means "to lean upon, or take hold of" ("camak,"
Hebrew #5564) It means to rest in and be sustained. Peace is a gift
that Jesus offers us to take us through any of life's circumstances.
Peace is what carries us above the storm and prevents it from
having power over us. This is why we praise, worship, dance, and
meditate. Let me remind you of the definition of the biblical word
peace ("shalowm," *Strong's* #7965): "Safe, happy, health, prosperity,
wellbeing, at rest, whole." I encourage you not to leave any part of
this out of your lives.

I honestly do not know where I would be today if I had not
learned to take every one of these forms of worship and put them to
work in my life. May I be so bold as to say that if you are leaving out
one of these commands to worship then you are missing a part of
the God kind of life that He so wants you to have? You are missing
an important tool that God provided for you to live a victorious life.
If you are a Word-only person who never participates in praise, I
encourage you to look thoroughly and honestly into what the Word
teaches about participating in praise. No, actually, I dare you!

The same goes for the people who love to praise and worship,
but have a real struggle being quiet before God or meditating on

His Word. You are missing a stabilizing force that gives power to your praise and worship. When you worship God, you put yourself in a position to hear His voice and receive wisdom and light, but if you are not in His Word, how can He reveal it?

We need balance. We need all God has offered us. We need His peace and all it carries.

> Hallelujah! Praise the Lord! Praise God in his
> holy sanctuary!
> Praise him in his stronghold in the sky!
> Praise him for his miracles of might!
> Praise him for his magnificent greatness!
> Praise him with the trumpets blasting!
> Praise him with the piano and guitar!
> Praise him with drums and dancing!
> Praise him with the loud, resounding clash
> of cymbals!
> Praise him with every instrument you can find!
> Let everyone everywhere join in the crescendo of
> ecstatic praise to Yahweh!
> Hallelujah! Praise the Lord! (Psalm 150, TPT)

CHAPTER 2

Encourage Yourself

> And David was greatly distressed; for the people spake of
> stoning him, because the soul of all the people was grieved,
> every man for his sons and for his daughters: but David
> encouraged himself in the Lord his God. —1 Samuel 30:6, KJV

I HAD A VERY DEAR PERSON IN MY LIFE WHO ASKED ME EVERY time I saw her, "Please pray for me that I will receive a touch from the Lord; I'm so dry." This concerned me very much and I did pray for her, but when we spoke about it, I could see clearly why she may have been so dry. I asked what she did each day to spend time with God. My friend seemed to be waiting for God to make the first move in filling her up with His presence so she could feel something and respond. This lady was sitting in "receive mode," and I suspect there are many in this situation, waiting for God to do something.

As we continued to speak about this, I tried to encourage my friend to participate in praise and worship at church. When I asked if she had any worship music at home, she said she did not. I know this sister loved the Lord and read her Bible, but obviously something was missing. Some people are hoping they can have hands laid on them in prayer and, poof! It's instantly all better. I am not saying that cannot happen from time to time when it's necessary, but it is not always God's way. He requires something from us.

As people with a mind and will, we decide to enter into God's presence and seek after Him. His Spirit is always with us, but we must actively commune with Him. I am sure you can all relate to this example. You are out and about and, by chance, run into someone you would consider a friend or acquaintance. In the course of the conversation they ask, "How come you never call me?" as if the relationship was all in your hands.

I have been in this situation and my first thought is, "The phone goes both ways." Why do people sit in receive mode, waiting for the other person to call first? I have had people complain to me that they have no friends, and that no one ever calls them to go out. My first response is, "Have you called them?" They look at me as if I am from outer space. I have learned that this attitude is very prevalent, and if I want to maintain a relationship with someone, I have to take responsibility and make the first effort myself. Sure, it's not fair, but I want the relationships.

I encourage you to have this attitude with God as David did. My example is not perfect, but you get my point. When you are in a bad situation go immediately to God and get for yourself the help and wisdom you need from His Word and presence. He will not do it for you.

Let's look at that word *encouraged* in *Strong's Concordance*. "Chazaq" means "to fasten upon, to seize (for fortification), to hold fast (with obstinance), to lean upon and lay hold of in a way that brings recovery, repair, and strength" (Hebrew #2388). It sounds like David meant business and knew what to do. I trust that you are also learning more and more about what to do.

I see from the Psalms that David's first go-to was to worship the Lord. We have already discussed this, but I will share one more scripture.

> Oh come, let us sing to the Lord! Let us shout
> joyfully to the Rock of our salvation. Let us come
> before His presence with thanksgiving; Let us
> shout joyfully to Him with psalms (Psalm 95:1,2).

I think David was in a position to encourage himself in the Lord because of his habit of praise but he also knew God's Word. He meditated on it day and night.

> Oh, how I love Your law! It is my meditation all
> the day (Psalm 119:97).

> My eyes are awake through the night
> watches, That I may meditate on Your word
> (Psalm 119:148).

I am by no means suggesting you spend all day and all night reading the Bible and praising God. Let's be honest; most of us are not in full-time ministry and have jobs and families. I am saying that we should take enough time to know what God says in His Word so that it comes to our remembrance when we need encouragement. When I was diagnosed with final-stage cancer, I knew enough to say, "I shall not die, but live, and declare the works of the Lord" (Psalm 118:17, KJV). I had to put that in so it could come out when I needed it. I wrote out what I did not know by heart so I could read it to myself and begin to plant it in my spirit. The most powerful words to bring encouragement are God's words and the most effective way to hear them is with your voice.

You do not need to be a full-time minister, spending hours a day in the Word and God's presence, to have this work for you. I certainly wasn't. I gave God priority and what time I could, and He met me there. God knows your life; He called you to it. You are just as anointed and equipped as any minister if you are doing what God called you to do. No one else can fulfill your role and call in God. It is essential to the body of Christ and unique to you. Someone needed to hear that.

When God's Word is in your heart, it makes you wise, which is a key to your response when trouble comes.

> You, through Your commandments, make me
> wiser than my enemies; for they are ever with me
> (Psalm 119:98).

> Wisdom is the most important thing; so get
> wisdom. If it costs everything you have, get
> understanding (Proverbs 4:7, NCV).

David knew how to respond when bad things happened. I am so glad that he was not perfect, though. He had initial reactions just like we do. He had his moments of crying, anger, and vengeful thoughts as we all do. When he finished his boohoo-ing though, he pulled up his big boy pants and called on the Lord, enabling him to do what was right. I love it when God shares the backstory, so we do not get the idea that these people were super perfect and above us. Many times in scripture, we also find David encouraging himself by looking at what God had done in the past. He rehearsed his victories, not his failures. This is one of my favorite scriptures where David stands up and boldly declares how it will be despite how it looks. He encourages himself with past victories and his confidence in God.

> But David said to Saul, "Your servant used to keep his father's sheep, and when a lion or a bear came and took a lamb out of the flock, I went out after it and struck it, and delivered *the lamb* from its mouth; and when it arose against me, I caught *it* by its beard, and struck and killed it. Your servant has killed both lion and bear; and this uncircumcised Philistine will be like one of them, seeing he has defied the armies of the living God." Moreover David said, "The LORD, who delivered me from the paw of the lion and from the paw of the bear, He will deliver me from the hand of this Philistine" (1 Samuel 17:34-37).

We can do this as well. Record it in a journal whenever you have a victory, no matter how small. I do this constantly, which is invaluable when I need to encourage myself. Take a few minutes now and reflect on any past prayer answers. Think back on any prophecies that may have been spoken over you that resounded in your spirit. Do you have a friend or family member who had a real breakthrough from God? All these things are evidence of God's power and faithfulness and can be a tool for stirring ourselves up as instructed in scripture (II Timothy 1:6).

Here are a couple of other scriptural directions for stirring ourselves up:

> Speaking to one another in psalms and hymns
> and spiritual songs, singing and making melody
> in your heart to the Lord (Ephesians 5:19).

> But you, dear friends, carefully build yourselves
> up in this most holy faith by praying in the Holy
> Spirit, staying right at the center of God's love,
> keeping your arms open and outstretched, ready
> for the mercy of our Master, Jesus Christ. This is
> the unending life, the real life! (Jude 20-21, MSG).

Here we see again the teaching of singing from our hearts and meditating on God and His Word. It is our lifeline. When we stir ourselves up as a daily habit and lifestyle, we can have the confidence that David did. What happened next when David remembered what God did with the lion and the bear? He cast all his care upon the Lord and ran at his giant with the Word of God in his mouth.

> Then David said to the Philistine, "You come to
> me with a sword, with a spear, and with a javelin.
> But I come to you in the name of the LORD of

hosts, the God of the armies of Israel, whom
you have defied. This day the LORD will deliver
you into my hand, and I will strike you and take
your head from you. And this day I will give the
carcasses of the camp of the Philistines to the
birds of the air and the wild beasts of the earth,
that all the earth may know that there is a God in
Israel. Then all this assembly shall know that the
LORD does not save with sword and spear; for the
battle *is* the Lord's, and He will give you into our
hands" (1 Samuel 17:45-47).

I love this passage because it reminds me a little of myself. I
often do some trash talking to the devil. *Are you going to mess with
me? Well, here's what's going to happen.*

David told the giant what would happen, and you know what?
It did, exactly how David said. (Keep in mind that this was a man
in the Old Covenant, a man who did not have the Spirit of God
living inside him. He did not even have the full written Word as
we do, but relied on the spoken word of the prophets.) This fact
should fill you with a lot of hope. This is the confidence we can
have in God. This is the result of encouraging yourself in the Lord,
the result of knowing Him.

I will end this chapter with our perfect example, Jesus himself,
and how He encouraged himself when facing the enemy.

Then Jesus was led up by the Spirit into the
wilderness to be tempted by the devil. And
when He had fasted forty days and forty nights,

afterward He was hungry. Now when the tempter came to Him, he said, "If You are the Son of God, command that these stones become bread."

But He answered and said, "It is written, 'Man shall not live by bread alone, but by every word that proceeds from the mouth of God.'"

Then the devil took Him up into the holy city, set Him on the pinnacle of the temple, and said to Him, "If You are the Son of God, throw Yourself down. For it is written:

'He shall give His angels charge over you,'

and,

'In their hands they shall bear you up,
Lest you dash your foot against a stone.'"

Jesus said to him, "It is written again, 'You shall not tempt the LORD your God.'"

Again, the devil took Him up on an exceedingly high mountain and showed Him all the kingdoms of the world and their glory. And he said to Him, "All these things I will give You if You will fall down and worship me."

Then Jesus said to him, "Away with you, Satan! For it is written, 'You shall worship the LORD your God, and Him only you shall serve.'"

Then the devil left Him, and behold, angels came and ministered to Him (Matthew 4:1-11).

Notice what Jesus spoke to the devil when answering him. He opposed and resisted him with God's Word only. Just as David did,

Jesus went after the giant with the Word in His mouth. Again, He had to have put that Word in Him to bring it out. Some may think, "But Jesus was God; how can I compare myself to how he acted?"

Let me help you with that. The Bible says Jesus studied the scriptures while a man on earth. He, in His humanity here on earth, had to learn and mature just like anyone else.

> And the Child grew and became strong in spirit,
> filled with wisdom; and the grace of God was
> upon Him (Luke 2:40).

> And Jesus increased in wisdom and stature, and
> in favor with God and men (Luke 2:52).

If someone "became" a certain way, it means they were not at the start. If someone "increases," then it means they started smaller; there was room to grow. The Bible also says in Hebrews 5:8 that Jesus learned obedience through the things he suffered. Sound familiar? This is why Jesus can be our perfect high priest who knows what it is like for us. He was in all ways tempted like we are. Jesus understands.

I encourage you to follow these godly examples and begin, if you have not already, to do something daily to encourage yourself in the Lord. Take responsibility for your own spiritual strength, maturity, joy, peace, and victory. No one can do it for you. YOU are the one who can confidently stand up in the face of adversity and send out those vibrations declaring, "This is what God says, and that's what I say." Watch the enemy flee!

CHAPTER 3

Ending Well

> But those who wait on the Lord
> Shall renew *their* strength;
> They shall mount up with wings like eagles,
> They shall run and not be weary,
> They shall walk and not faint. —Isaiah 40:31

I SAW A PROFOUND POST ON SOCIAL MEDIA A LITTLE WHILE AGO that I needed to share on these pages. The analogy showed an interaction between an eagle and a crow. Crows are one of the only birds that will dare attack an eagle. They do so because they travel in packs and eagles are generally solitary. The crow may even jump on the eagle's back and try and peck at it. Since the eagle cannot fight a whole pack of crows or reach the one on its back, it simply flies to its extremely high place in the sky where no other bird can. The crows cannot attain that place.

Reading that reminded me so much of our position in the Spirit. When the enemy, the crow, is pestering you, trying to discourage you, or accusing you, simply begin to worship God and go to your place in the Spirit where the enemy cannot function or stay. Get out of his turf. If we can learn this, we will be unstoppable. It will frustrate the enemy to no end when he gets praise and worship back in his face whenever he tries to speak to you. He hates it and will run every time, leaving us in our place of peace.

In this chapter, I want to talk about our motivation for doing things God's way, keeping our eye on the prize, so to speak. There is a planned end for God's people as well as for the ultimate enemy of God and his people. God's plan for how we "end up" is daily, short-term, and long-term. Daily obedience and submission to God keep us on track with His longer-term plans for us. Knowing this will encourage us along our way and help keep us focused. God only has good plans for us (Jeremiah 29:11),[6] which are achievable daily.

Some of you have had prophecies spoken over you, perhaps a long time ago, and you have not seen them fulfilled. I can relate because I have had them. I am not talking about everyone who says, "Thus saith the Lord." Let's face it; there is a lot of that going on. I am talking about accurate prophecies from anointed ministers that resonated deep in your spirit. You knew it was God. I encourage you to hold onto these as God's intended end for you. Do not give up because of time or circumstances.

Think about David and the words spoken over him. After he was anointed by the prophet and told he was the future king, he went right back to tending the sheep. Not only that, but he was chased, hunted, plotted against, ridiculed, and exiled for many years till he saw that fulfilled. You do understand that the enemy heard those prophecies too? He immediately sets himself to stealing them from you, to get you to lose hope. I want to encourage you to pull those out, dust them off, and begin to believe God again. It had been many years of hardship, adversity, pain, and downright discouragement for me as well, but I am now seeing God's plan unfold. I have become wiser in the things of God, how to operate "In Him," and I am sharing this with you.

> *I would have lost heart,* unless I had believed that I
> would see the goodness of the Lord
> In the land of the living (Psalm 27:13).

> You prepare a table before me in the presence of
> my enemies (Psalm 23:5).

Your Wealthy Place

> We went through fire and through water: but thou
> broughtest us out into a wealthy place (Psalm
> 66:12, KJV).

This verse is very meaningful to me because I indisputably went through the fire and the water. The enemy has tried to take me out through severe depression, the agony of divorce, and, to top it all off, bone marrow cancer in the final stage. Each of us has our own story, but the point of it all is to go through it. You can come out on the other side to your wealthy place in God. We are not meant to have the devil win over us. Jesus paid too high a price. David knew the fire and the water more than any of us, but he also "saw" his wealthy place in God. He believed God's Word and set his eyes and heart to His promises, His end.

Let's look at the word wealthy: "rvayah" means "drunk, full, satiate, satisfy, soak, running over" (*Strong's* #7310). Does that sound good to you? That is God's plan for you every day. We are meant to live in Him to the point that we are so full, so satisfied, so running over with His presence that nothing affects us. We can live above the fray. Another related scripture is Isaiah 43:1-2:

> But now, thus says the Lord, who created you,
>> O Jacob,
> And He who formed you, O Israel:
> "Fear not, for I have redeemed you;
> I have called *you* by your name;
> You *are* Mine.
> When you pass through the waters, I will be
>> with you;
> And through the rivers, they shall not overflow you.
> When you walk through the fire, you shall not
>> be burned,
> Nor shall the flame scorch you."

Here we see again that we will go through some fire and water. We should not be surprised or offended by this. The world is full of trouble, even for the righteous. What we need to remember is that God is with us, we are His, and these things are powerless to overcome us when we live in God. I love the last line. To me, it means that we won't even smell like smoke. It means that there will be no remaining evidence on us that we ever went through the trial. For me on my journey, that means no side effects, no tiredness, no maintenance therapy, no neuropathy, and no relapses. It means I come out whole. That is MY place, MY end.

It's a Trap

Have you ever been in a situation where you wanted to "help" God along toward what you want or things that were spoken over you because it doesn't seem to be going right? Perhaps someone is trying to come against you, or it is taking too long and you have a great idea.

If anyone was ever tempted and had the opportunity to take matters into his own hands, it was David. On two different occasions, he had the chance to strike down King Saul, the man who was hunting him down and trying to kill him. His men who were with him encouraged him to do so. David, however, knew God better than that. David obeyed God's principles and by doing so kept God operating on his behalf right through to the victory and the fulfillment of his promises. Have you ever stopped to think about what would have happened if David had taken the opportunity to kill Saul himself? To answer that, we only have to look to the story of David and Bathsheba. Here, David did take matters into his own hands and the entire history of Israel changed—not for good. In this account recorded in II Samuel 11 and 12, we see the results of David's murderous act. God said that the sword would never depart from his house, and we see that his entire reign was consumed with war.

I often wonder why David obeyed God the first time and then took matters into his own hands the second time. We will never know, but I am thankful for the lesson and the fact that God will use us despite our failures. We all fail; I know I have, but failure isn't final. Just repent like David did and start again. David was still the man after God's own heart. He was still anointed and he recovered. He ended well.

Taking matters into our own hands is always a trap set by the enemy. I taught this concept in my first book. If you have it in your mind to do something to defend yourself or retaliate against an offense, stop for a moment and follow your actions to the next step and then the next. Follow the possible consequences and outcomes in the natural without even bringing God's consequences into it. That will be enough to give you pause, but then think about how you will be tying God's hands from intervening on your behalf and bringing to pass what you are believing for.

It's time for another of Marion's confessions. Confession is so good for the soul, isn't it? Especially when it is coming from someone else. In my first book, I spoke of some difficult situations in my new marriage, as we were both older, set in our ways, and had a lot of hurtful baggage from our first marriages. My imagination was getting carried away with all kinds of notions (the cancer drugs didn't help) and I stooped to the low point of snooping to try and "prove" my notions. If you have been involved in any such behavior, I want you to listen to me very carefully.

At the time, as much of a mess as I was, I was praying for my marriage and believing in God for change. There were some very real issues that I knew only God could influence. In my desperation and immaturity, I took matters into my own hands because I thought I just needed to know some things. I became obsessed with "checking" for results. In reality though, what I was doing was searching for evidence to the contrary, proof that things were not changing. Does that sound as ridiculous to you as it now does to me? I hope so.

Let's carry those actions through like I spoke of above. If a person who believes God for something in their marriage (or in any relationship) goes checking for evidence, what happens if you find it? First, you have demonstrated that you do not honestly believe God is working in your situation. Second, you have searched out something to fuel your doubt instead of your faith. Third, you have put yourself in a position where you now have to deal with that knowledge in your mind and imagination, possibly harming yourself and your cause even more.

Now let's look at what it means if you check and do not find anything. Does it mean God was working and He gets the glory? Don't fool yourself. This shows that your faith was in what you found in the natural, not in your belief in God. This does nothing to build a faith foundation or a "lion and bear" legacy that builds you up for your subsequent victories.

This behavior is a playground for the devil to destroy you as you have stepped onto his playing field, his turf. You have tied God's hands and stepped out of your place. I have learned the hard way that looking at what *is* will do nothing but steal your confidence, hope, and belief. I am not saying we should stick our heads in the sand and pretend things are not there. That would be foolish. We need correct information to make a faith stand.

I am saying that once you have all the facts and determine what you are believing God for, stand on that with determination. See it in your imagination the way you are believing and do not go looking for things that will hurt your faith and your result.

Through these experiences and what I have learned, Hebrews 11:1 has become so alive to me. I will attempt to paraphrase it in my own words as I have received it from the Holy Spirit This is how I now treat everything I am believing God for:

My absolute unshakable belief in what I am asking from God is the sure, bedrock foundation that holds up what I have set on it. It is its substance and the assurance from God that gives me absolute confidence. It is the proof that cannot be denied and gives me the certainty that I have it even though I have not physically seen it yet.[7]

I have learned that my faith only works when I treat it this way because it IS that way. My unshakable faith is what makes it happen. My pit-bull determination that God will do what I ask if I am in line with Him and doing it His way IS the stuff that answered prayer is made of. I walk around now just acting like it's so because it is. I speak it, imagine it, and, to the best of my ability, respond like it's already done. This means I do not even give a thought to any other reality. When I find myself straying, I get into His presence for a reset, then take myself by the scruff of the neck and talk to myself. My end will be as I see it in God's Word. End of story.

> For assuredly, I say to you, whoever says to this
> mountain, 'Be removed and be cast into the sea,'
> and does not doubt in his heart, but believes that
> those things he says will be done, he will have
> whatever he says (Mark 11:23)

Not Even Smoke

When I read that phrase in Isaiah 43:2, "nor shall the flame scorch you," I always think of the three men in the fiery furnace from Daniel 3:27:

> They saw these men on whose bodies the fire had
> no power; the hair of their head was not singed
> nor were their garments affected, and the smell of
> fire was not on them.

Because of their unwavering faith in God, they came out of their fiery trial with not even one piece of evidence on them that they had even been in the fire. All it did was build their faith legacy for the next situation. This is a lesson we also learn in the life of David. Time and time again, when he obeys God, we see him winning battle after battle and recovering all.

The best example of this is found in the story of Ziklag in I Samuel 30, which we have looked at before. At the time, this was David's hometown, and his wives and children were there while he and his men went to war. When they returned after the battle, they found that the city was burned, and all the women and children were gone. I am sure he was the same as all of us in crying out to God: WHY? No one can answer that question, but what is recorded gives us hope and shows God's ways.

No matter how bad it looks or how unfair the situation is, God's plan is for you to recover all and for nothing to be missing; nothing broken. If God looks down at the wicked and laughs (Psalm 37:13), then we should not worry about it. David not only recovered all his people, but he got all the plunder that the enemy had gathered from their battles. This sounds like a great setup to me. He got double for his trouble.

We have to remember when things come against us, who it is that is on our side. God is our avenger, and He does a great job all by Himself.

> And shall God not avenge His own elect who cry
> out day and night to Him, though He bears long
> with them? I tell you that He will avenge them
> speedily (Luke 18:7-8).

> For You have maintained my right and my cause;
> You sat on the throne judging in righteousness
> (Psalm 9:4).

We looked at these scriptures in my first book, and I present these to God regularly. If I have a godly cause and I have His Word to back me up, then I can put my faith in this. I never want to get in God's way of avenging me for what has been stolen. God takes our welfare very seriously. The book of Psalms in particular talks about the end for the wicked and it's not pretty. There are twenty-nine direct references in scripture about the punishment of the wicked and their end.

David cried out to God many times about the seeming prosperity of the wicked, because it bothered him, as I am sure it does you. I have found a way to deal with this and I hope it helps you. Let's look first at what God showed David in Psalm 73:16-19.

> When I thought *how* to understand this,
> It *was* too painful for me—
> Until I went into the sanctuary of God;
> *Then* I understood their end.

> Surely You set them in slippery places;
> You cast them down to destruction.
> Oh, how they are *brought* to desolation, as in
> a moment!
> They are utterly consumed with terrors.

If you understand their end compared to yours, you can almost feel sorry for them, and you should. I think of people who let the enemy control or use them like puppets on a string. They are blind spiritually and have no idea how they are being used and manipulated. They have no idea how the devil is laughing at them and are oblivious to their terrifying end. This knowledge is not meant to give us satisfaction, but to evoke compassion and prayer. We can respond in love and obedience to God by understanding what is happening. We never wish this on anyone or rejoice in it, because doing so would take you out of your place in God where your prayers are answered. We are told to bless those who curse you for a reason (Matthew 5:44).[8] This is for your benefit and to keep you in victory. Look at this in Proverbs 24:17-18:

> Do not rejoice when your enemy falls,
> And do not let your heart be glad when
> he stumbles;
> Lest the LORD see *it,* and it displease Him,
> And He turn away His wrath from him.

Staying in love may not change their end, but it will guarantee yours. Love is God's only commandment, through which everything He has for us works. David's end was a complete victory despite his mistakes, because he always sought after God and kept his heart right.

After all I have been through, I have also learned how it ends when you do things God's way.[9] I am so much closer to God now and have found my purpose. The trials that were meant to destroy me were turned around by God to make me a force for Him. Sometimes I can even be thankful for them (I did say *sometimes!*), because of the changes in me. He taught me how because I relentlessly pursued Him in my desperation. Keep your eye on the end game; keep your eyes on Him. It does not ever have to be over for us despite what it may look like in the middle. God's Word is sure and can be counted on always.

> *Never doubt* God's mighty power to work in you and accomplish all this. He will achieve infinitely more than your greatest request, your most unbelievable dream, and exceed your wildest imagination! He will outdo them all, for his miraculous power constantly energizes you. Now we offer up to God all the glorious praise that rises from every church in every generation through Jesus Christ—and all that will yet be manifest through time and eternity. Amen (Ephesians 3:20-21, TPT).

SECTION 2

The Spirit in You

For God has not given us a spirit of fear, but
of power and of love and of a sound mind.
—II Timothy 1:7

CHAPTER 4

Spirit of Power

Behold, I give unto you power to tread on serpents and
scorpions, and over all the power of the enemy: and nothing
shall by any means hurt you. —Luke 10:19, KJV

WE CANNOT BEGIN TO SPEAK ABOUT OUR AUTHORITY
without first establishing the scriptural basis of that
authority. If you have read the book of Ephesians, you will notice
that the first three chapters are all about who you are and what
God has put in you. It is like a cheerleading session to lead you
into and empower you for what He is going to require of you
in the last three chapters. God never expects you to do His
will without first giving you the backing and tools you need to
accomplish it.

In the verse above we see the word power. The first mention
is about us and is "exousia," meaning "force, capacity, mastery
(superhuman), delegated influence, authority, and strength"
(*Strong's* #1849). The second mention refers to the enemy's

power as "the ability to exercise force, strength, and deeds only" ("dunamis," *Strong's* #1411). There is no mention of any authority or influence. Both definitions talk about strength and ability, but only we have authority from God to override our opponents' strength. We do not have to be intimidated.

This reminds me of a story I once heard. When a police officer stands in traffic and holds up his hand, all vehicles in front of him stop. Is he physically stronger than these trucks and buses? No. They could easily run him over if not for the authority he carries. To ignore that authority would carry serious consequences. It is not a perfect example, but you get my point. As God's children, we have been given a position of authority and do not have to fight with the enemy on his turf, by his rules, or let him run us around with his devices.

> … Jesus Christ, the faithful witness, the firstborn
> from the dead, and the ruler over the kings of
> the earth.
> To Him who loved us and washed us from
> our sins in His own blood and has made us kings
> and priests to His God and Father, to Him *be*
> glory and dominion forever and ever. Amen
> (Revelation 1:5-6).

> But you are a chosen generation, a royal
> priesthood, a holy nation, His own special
> people, that you may proclaim the praises of
> Him who called you out of darkness into His
> marvelous light (I Peter 2:9).

Kings and Priests

This power we have comes from our dual anointing as priests and kings before God. Pay close attention because understanding this will give you confidence in approaching God and in everything you face in your life. We are in a tremendous position to attain victory every day of our lives.

Consider the priests in the Old Testament. They were the only ones allowed to go behind the veil into the Holy of Holies, the presence of God. Because of Jesus, that veil has been torn down and we now have direct access. Let me paint a picture for you. The priests, as described in the book of Exodus, had special washings, a special robe, a belt, a breastplate, a holy crown, and anointing oil poured over them. Let's take each one and see how we are now equipped the same way.

Special Washings
To Him who loved us and washed us from our
sins in His own blood (Revelation 1:5).

We have been washed in a special way to make us clean before God. Our sins have been washed away forever by Jesus' blood. Unlike the priests, we do not have to get washed over and over. We are permanently clean by the one sacrifice of Jesus. Praise God.

A Special Robe
I will greatly rejoice in the Lord, my soul shall be
joyful in my God; For He has clothed me with the
garments of salvation, He has covered me with

the robe of righteousness, as a bridegroom decks
himself with ornaments, and as a bride adorns
herself with her jewels (Isaiah 61:10).

We have a robe as well, the robe of the righteousness of Jesus.
We are covered by the position of being right with God. Jesus
made us right with God the same way we have been justified (just
as if I'd never sinned) before God. This is an amazing thing, and
we get to receive it as a gift.

A Belt and a Breastplate

So stand up and do not be moved. Wear a belt
of truth around your body. Wear a piece of iron
over your chest which is being right with God
(Ephesians 6:14, NLV).

What is our belt of truth? It is the Word of God. When we
know the truth (by applying it to our lives) it will set us free (John
8:37). Knowing is doing, not just nice words in a book on the table.
Our breastplate of iron is the fact that we are right with God. No
arrows of the enemy can penetrate that plate. He cannot take that
fact away from us no matter how hard he tries.

A Holy Crown

For You have made him a little lower than
the angels,
And You have crowned him with glory and honor
(Psalm 8:5).

And the glory which You gave Me I have given
them, that they may be one just as We are one
(John 17:22).

This is a tough one for some Christians, especially those
who have false humility and do not fully realize who Christ has
made them. I love this verse, because it shows a picture of how
much we are one with Christ. This word, glory is "doxa" and
means "dignity, glor(-ious), honor" (Strong's #1391). The base
word means to be "accounted ... [to] be of reputation as such, or
thought of" (#1380). Let me make it simple: God sees us just like
He sees Jesus because Jesus gave us that gift. We have been made
the righteousness of God in Him, Christ Jesus (I Corinthians
5:21, KJV), and positionally there is no difference. These are
powerful truths and I encourage you to study them on your own.
It will change your life.

An Anointing

But you have an anointing from the Holy One,
and you know all things... But the anointing
which you have received from Him abides in you,
and you do not need that anyone teach you; but
as the same anointing teaches you concerning
all things, and is true, and is not a lie, and just as
it has taught you, you will abide in Him (I John
2:20, 27).

Now He who establishes us with you in Christ
and has anointed us is God (II Corinthians 1:21).

I think the anointing is the greatest picture of our priesthood, because it represents the Holy Spirit upon us and in us. The word is "chrisma" and means "smearing or endowment" of the Holy Spirit *(Strong's* #5545). I am sure we have all heard the phrase, "The oil of the Holy Spirit." His presence is with us always and is our seal and guarantee (II Corinthians 1:22).[10] He is the one through whom we have fellowship with God and have the power to live for Him in this world.

When the priests were anointed, the oil was poured over their heads and flowed down over their whole bodies. They were covered with it, and they knew they had been anointed. We lose that picture in our culture, because we see a little bottle and the oil applied to the forehead only. It is challenging to get the all-consuming meaning from a dab. When we are in Christ, the Holy Spirit is poured in and is with us always.

Now that we have a picture of our priestly anointing, let's look at the priest's activities so we can understand what we are to do in our position. One of the priest's main activities was to enter the Holy of Holies and make atonement for themselves and the people's sins. He approached God on behalf of others. The priests would know God's Word and activate it for the benefit of the people. Our priestly anointing is also for the benefit of others and ourselves. We are commanded to pray for all men (I Timothy 2:1) and our prayers have great power. Look at this scripture.

> Confess your trespasses to one another, and pray
> for one another, that you may be healed. The
> effective, fervent prayer of a righteous man avails
> much (James 5:16).

As priests before God, we have access to the throne. We have the ministry of lifting people and situations before God and bringing power and anointing to accomplish what God wants according to His Word. We have the ability and the right to present God's Word back to Him in faith-filled prayers and expect to see things change.

Now, let's take a look at the kingly anointing. Just picture in your mind what you think a king is either in today's world or in times past. Myself, I picture someone with supreme authority. This is someone who makes commands and is obeyed immediately. A king rules and dominates.

Did you imagine something like that? There are kings of very differing character. Some are cruel and self-seeking while others care about and serve their people, but the authority does not change. When they speak, the hearer responds. To disregard would hold serious consequences. Why is that? They have been given authority, a foundation, and a foothold of power by the country they represent. They have official documents to show who they are. You know where I'm going, right?

> Then God said, "Let Us make man in Our image, according to Our likeness; let them have dominion over the fish of the sea, over the birds of the air, and over the cattle, over all the earth and over every creeping thing that creeps on the earth" (Genesis 1:26).

> He raised us up with Christ the exalted One, *and we ascended with him into the glorious perfection*

> *and authority* of the heavenly realm, for we are
> now co-seated as one with Christ! (Ephesians
> 2:6, TPT).

Here we see that God created man to have dominion over everything on the earth. Man lost that authority and dominion, which is why Jesus had to come and restore it. We were, however, originally created in His image and a position of dominion. In the second passage we see that now, in Christ, we are seated again with Him in a position of authority in the heavens. Christ has given us back our authority. The passage I get very excited about, though, is Genesis 2:7 because, when you search it out in Hebrew, you will find that it means God created us a speaking spirit, just like Him.

> And the Lord God formed man of the dust of the
> ground, and breathed into his nostrils the breath
> of life, and man became a living soul (Genesis
> 2:7, KJV).

This is a fascinating and eye-opening study, which I will not get into here, but you can get great information at torahisteaching. com/man-is-a-speaking-spirit. God created everything by His words. The beginning of the book of Genesis repeats over and over, "Then God said ... and it was so." The passage in scripture where God tells us "say to this mountain" and "He will have whatever he says" (Mark 11:23-24)[11] makes so much sense since we are speaking spirits created in His image and have authority. Also related to this is II Corinthians 4:13: "And since we have the same spirit of faith, according to what is written, 'I believed and therefore I spoke,' we also believe and therefore speak."

The fact that we speak out of our mouths what we believe from God's Word, and that we speak it out from our place of authority in Him is our kingly anointing in action. Let's put both of our anointings together to see how it works in our daily lives.

As priests before God, we come boldly to the throne of grace (Hebrews 4:16) and can ask in confidence for our own and others' needs when we return His Word to Him in faith. We believe God's Word and we pray out those words.

Let's say you have a child who is straying away from what you have taught them and is starting to dabble in some dangerous behavior. As a priest before God, you can go before the throne of grace and return God's Word to Him that says, "All your children shall be taught by the Lord, and great shall be the peace of your children" (Isaiah 54:13). Since you believe this scripture with all your heart you can then turn around and boldly declare out into the atmosphere, to the devil, or to whoever else needs to be told that they cannot have your child and they will return to the Lord. That is the priestly and kingly anointing working together. This will work in anything you believe for that has scripture to back it up. This is what I did when I stood up and refused to die. The enemy cannot resist your bold vibrations in the spirit. He has to flee (James 4:7). He has to listen to authority—it is a spiritual law.

I can sense already that you are getting bolder and wiser, and you are not going to let the devil run you around with circumstances. I can almost feel your heart beginning to burn and the light going on. Start practicing this, if you have not already, with something small and you will watch your faith grow. The truth will set you free, my friends.

Authority In Action

Another simple way of picturing the principles above is to think of your backing that allows you to stand, the position that will enable you to act. Knowing the process and the reason behind it gives you confidence if you are anything like me. The more I receive the revelation God has given in His Word regarding His ways the more powerful I become. This is good news for you because you can do this too. This is a level playing field. God never has been, and never will be, a respecter of persons (Acts 10:34). He loves you as much as He loves anyone else and even as much as He loves Jesus (John 17:23).[12]

I remember a time when I was still hurting very much from the trauma of cancer and the other difficulties in my life. I was beginning to get these principles down in my spirit and put them into practice. I was believing God for changes, but often did not go about it the right way. I have spoken before of my nagging, shaming, reasoning, and sometimes yelling, to demand my rights and position. As we all know, none of these things work in any situation in the long term. One morning I took some oil and went to my husband's side of the bed. I found some scriptures that backed up the things I was believing for in my marriage, and I prayed these scriptures before God and anointed his pillow. This was very much the priestly anointing in action (although I don't think I fully realized it at the time). There was even oil involved as a point of contact.

After I did this, as is my practice, I went about worshiping God and dancing in my living room. As I was doing so, I started speaking out and taking authority over any familiar spirits that may have been influencing my home. I demanded that they leave, and I know I felt a certain power in my spirit. Remember those vibrations I spoke of earlier? I believe this is what was happening at that time. I was addressing the spirits behind the situation, not the person. I have never stopped dealing with things this way. Nothing is too small for you to take authority over. This needs to become our lifestyle. This is your superior weapon in the spirit that works every time.

There is a scene in one of the Indiana Jones movies—Raiders of the Lost Ark—that comes to mind whenever I think of this authority and position. Do you remember when Indy faced an attack from an expert swordsman? He jumps in front of Indy and starts dancing around, waving his huge sword skillfully and threateningly while screaming. This goes on for a while and it looks like Indy might be in trouble. As the swordsman starts to charge at him, Indy calmly takes out his gun and shoots the man. There was no struggle, no wrestling, no crying or fretting. As big, loud, and showy as the swordsman was, Indy's weapon was superior. He "tread" on him.[13] Are you getting the picture here? As big, loud, and full of smoke and mirrors as the devil may be, your weapon is superior. He cannot fight you in your position in the Spirit. He must fall to those who know their authority. Indy may have used a gun, but your weapon is exercised by your mouth. Because we are speaking spirits created in the image of our Father God, we speak His Word just as He does.

I know there are many good and bad ideas concerning the teaching of being created in God's image and, as His children, operating the way He does. I want to illustrate with a picture to help you understand and live in this beautiful gift we have. I have a daughter that is so much a clone of me that it's almost unbelievable.

She looks like me, talks like me, and thinks like me. I can generally predict what she is going to do because I know what I was like at her age. She has my temper, a lot of my likes and dislikes, my impatience, and many of my good qualities. How did she get to be so much like me? She was born to me and spent much time around me. Is she my equal? Well, yes and no.

She is my "kind," because she is my offspring. She is not inferior as a human being in any way. She operates on this earth the same as I do with a mind, a mouth, two arms and legs, and a heart. I did not produce offspring that has telepathy, anti-gravity capabilities, or the ability to wiggle her nose and make things appear. Neither did I produce offspring that is of lesser value, lesser mental function, or lesser skills. I duplicated what is within my kind. She is not my equal in her position in the family and level of knowledge and experience. I will always be her mother and older and wiser. Sometimes I cringe because I see the mistakes she is about to make; I have been there. I can try and warn her or offer advice, but she has her own mind to think with. I will never try to make her subservient because she is of equal value with the ability to choose. My position above her is one of headship and respect as is her father's. She will never be my mom.

This is not a perfect example, but it is very much like we are created in our Father's image. When we are born again, we are born of the Spirit and instantly changed into a new creature spiritually and placed in Christ. We are returned to our original place in creation. Did God create inferior offspring? No. He created the same kind that operates the same way. We learn, grow, and become more like Him by being around and imitating Him. Hopefully, we will listen to His Word and make the right choices.

We will never be equal to Him in that He will always be our Father and above us in His perfection and headship. We will always be the child. I hope that helps some.

Because our Father demonstrated to us that He created this world by speaking words, I implore you never to stay silent. I think too many Christians stop at praying (the priestly anointing) and never go on to the next step of commanding God's Word to be done on the earth. Jesus only spoke of seeing great faith a couple of times in the Bible. One of those times was in Matthew 8:8-10:

> The centurion answered and said, "Lord, I am not
> worthy that You should come under my roof. But
> only speak a word, and my servant will be healed.
> For I also am a man under authority, having
> soldiers under me. And I say to this *one,* 'Go,' and
> he goes; and to another, 'Come,' and he comes;
> and to my servant, 'Do this,' and he does *it.*"
>
> When Jesus heard *it,* He marveled, and
> said to those who followed, "Assuredly, I say to
> you, I have not found such great faith, not even
> in Israel!"

This centurion understood the power of words spoken with authority in the natural world and the spiritual. He knew that Jesus only had to give the command and the sickness had to leave. Operating this principle is faith in action. Jesus called it "great faith." Your world and the world around you are waiting on what you are going to say, and what you are going to command in His name (Romans 8:19).[14] They are waiting for us to get a revelation of who we are in Christ and start operating in it. Angels are listening for the voice of His Word (Psalm 103:20) so they can perform it and you can be sure the enemy is watching for those vibrations. Don't waste your time and energy playing the devil's game. Stand in confidence with your superior weapon and let God fight your battle.

CHAPTER 5

Spirit of Love

And this hope is not a disappointing fantasy, because we can now
experience the endless love of God cascading into our hearts
through the Holy Spirit who lives in us. —Romans 5:5, TPT

I HAVE BEEN GOING THROUGH A 365-DAY DEVOTIONAL FOR THE
last couple of months that is completely devoted to the subject
of God's love. It is wonderful and I am getting so much out of it,
but there is one recurring theme I am noticing, and I'll bet you
have seen it in many devotionals, Christian articles, and sermons.
It is a thought process that is meant well and sounds good, but in
reality, can be the thing tripping us up and leaving us discouraged
and feeling like a failure. Sometimes I wonder if those who write
these well-meaning teachings realize what they are saying. I have
caught myself getting wrapped up in it because it sounds so right.

These teaching often start with the phrase, "You must." Even
this wonderful devotional used this phrase in teaching that you
must make a quality decision to walk in love and respond the way

Jesus would. In another section is the teaching that you must put down your flesh and control your temper. Here are a few others you may have heard being taught for great and biblical reasons.

- You must forgive or you will not be forgiven.
- You must watch your words.
- You must turn the other cheek.
- You must be humble.
- You must (oh, how I do not like this one) be patient.

All these teachings are correct, right? They are all taught in the Bible and are the characteristics of the Christian life. Would it surprise you if I said I did not even try to be any of those things? Notice the words "I" and "try." This is the key and my point. The problem is that many people try to do these things with their own effort. They grit their teeth and determine that they will do the right thing. They wake up in the morning, read their chapter, say a quick prayer for God's help and guidance throughout the day, then try to obey what they have been taught. I am not criticizing these people; I have been there myself.

Just Like Daddy

We all want to do what is right and obey God's Word, but what a lot of us lack is the revelation that we don't have to do it alone. We cannot do it alone and were never meant to. If you are having trouble on a day-to-day basis with making correct decisions and responding in a godly way, then I encourage you to spend more time in His presence. Love is the natural outflow from spending time with God, because you are becoming more like Him. I am sure you have heard this warning, perhaps from your mother: "Be careful who you hang around with because you will become just like them." It's very true and it also works in the positive.

I will add one more to my "You musts" list that we have heard many times: "You must be careful of what you say and do, because God is always with you and knows everything." I remember it being used almost as a threat. Any of these can be a form of intimidation to get someone to perform according to another's standards even though it may not be intended. Again, it is self-effort and fear based. This is the wrong perspective. Yes, God is always with you. His love is always with you, changing you from the inside out. He is guiding you in your daily life, not so that YOU will be more diligent and perform better, but because there will be more of Him in you to affect your everyday life and decision-making. You are made in God's image, and He is love. He is made out of love. That's why He's so good at it. You are made out of the same thing in your spirit and operate optimally when you walk that way.

I am reminded of an analogy I learned at my day job. Have you ever read warning labels on products saying, "Only warrantied for intended use"? This means that if you operate the product in an unintended way, it will not work correctly or receive the benefit of the warranty. My pastor gives the example of rowing a canoe with a guitar. It will work, but it's not the optimal use for that guitar. You are designed to operate best in God's kingdom when full of His love and peace. It is the only work or striving we are ever told to do.

> Let us therefore be diligent to enter that rest, lest
> anyone fall according to the same example of
> disobedience (Hebrews 4:11).

When we get in His presence there is joy and peace and that will cause us to live a better life. It is a natural outflow of Him and that is all that counts. This needs to be our priority as it will affect everything we do. Without His presence, the things mentioned above are often just religious activity and, as we see in I Corinthians 13, have no real profit.

> Though I speak with the tongues of men and of angels, but have not love, I have become sounding brass or a clanging cymbal. And though I have *the gift of* prophecy, and understand all mysteries and all knowledge, and though I have all faith, so that I could remove mountains, but have not love, I am nothing. And though I bestow all my goods to feed *the poor,* and though I give my body to be burned, but have not love, it profits me nothing (I Corinthians 13:1-3).

There are some Christians who don't seem to struggle in this area. They have no problem understanding how much God loves them and can receive it and give it away. I look at people like that and, to be honest, I am somewhat envious. This is not the case with me at all. I never grew up knowing how to love and I cannot relate. My first inkling of love came to me when I was a young woman of twenty-five holding my first child. The emotion was foreign to me. My love for my children was fierce and protective. It did not develop much outside of my children. If you are like me and never really developed in love, there is no condemnation. We need to get in God's presence more than sweet sister or brother so-and-so. There is nothing wrong with that. Remember that God chose you knowing your personality and limitations. There is a purpose for you as you are. Perhaps sweet little Christian so-and-so could not do what you are called to do because it requires really tough skin. Perhaps your calling requires standing up in front of adversity and not caring what people think. Maybe you will be on the front-firing lines where you get stoked by the action. Perhaps you will be required to deal with controversial issues and get much criticism. You would not want to be a softie in those cases. We are all different and perfectly suited to our callings.

Think about that before you judge yourself or anyone else. I don't mean to suggest we do not try and improve our dispositions; just don't think you are less than someone who seems the perfect Christian. Trust me, you may be surprised about what is behind closed doors. Remember that God's Word says, "Not many wise, not many noble or mighty are called" (I Corinthians 1:26). In other words, we qualify. We need to stop beating ourselves up for our so-called flaws and realize that those flaws may be an asset. If I was so perfect, perhaps God could not use me. I think of this often when I am going through trials or corrections and say to myself as a paraphrase of the Apostle Paul, "Lest I get a fat head" (see II Corinthians 12:7).[15] A position of needing to cling to Jesus is not a bad thing. Remember that we are all just gloves that God puts His hand in.

Do not confuse the action of love with feelings. You do not have to be a sweet little puffball to be operating in love (thank you, Jesus). Sometimes Jesus was pretty tough on people, and He was perfect. You can even love people by faith until it comes to pass in your spirit. What matters is getting in God's presence through His Word and worship until you get a revelation of just how much He loves you so that you reflect His image more and more.

The Motive

Have you ever wondered why love is the only command in the new covenant?

> A new commandment I give to you, that you love
> one another; as I have loved you, that you also
> love one another (John 13:34).

As a second witness, I will ask you to look up I John 2:7-11,[16] as it fully explains this new commandment.

There were hundreds of rules and regulations in the Old Covenant. So many that no one could ever keep them all. Even the Ten Commandments alone would have been a lot of pressure if left to ourselves. The love of God in our hearts is the only thing that could even begin to steer us in the right direction. Remember, the saints in the Old Covenant had the Spirit of God upon them from time to time, not in them. No wonder these rules were impossible, and they failed so often. Examining each of these commandments will show why love is the answer. If I love my neighbor, I will not steal from them or lie to them. I certainly would not kill them. If I love God I will not curse with His name or be looking for something else to worship or take first place in my life. Love is the answer to all things and why we are commanded to enter into His love. Love is how the Kingdom of God, and everything offered in it, works. You cannot love yourself without the love of God and you cannot operate your faith. I will look at love's role in living by faith for this teaching.

I learned this lesson the hard way a couple of years ago when I desperately needed a mountain to be moved. I had a dire situation that involved a person being a painful thorn in my side. It was so bad that it seemed my life could be ruined over it. I knew the teaching of "speaking to the mountains" in Mark 11:23 and had even taught about it in Bible School. I was putting my faith and my speaking toward this situation for over a year to no avail before I realized that I had been practically cursing this person with my attitude. I had been letting venom come out of my mouth towards them.

No wonder my faith was not working. When I realized this, I repented and asked God what to do. Through this situation, I learned what operating in the love of God looked like. It was not ooey-gooey or full of feelings as some think love is. I did not like this person and I did not have to. All I needed to do was find a way to sincerely bless them while commanding the situation to change. That's what I did. I asked God to bless them with their dream job and much happiness ... far away from here. This may bring up two responses. First, how could you pray for their promotion and happiness when they have been such trouble to you? The second, aren't you praying selfishly by saying they should move far from here?

To answer this, we need to understand what real, Christ-like agape love is. You can be angry with someone, state the problem, and still be in biblical love. Let me give you an example. Have you ever been so angry with your spouse or close friend and your feelings so wounded that it almost physically hurt? I am sure we all have. So, when you felt like that, did you refuse to cook dinner for them? Did you throw their belongings out the window? Did you cancel the vacation and say they deserved it? Did you refuse to provide for their needs? Did you shut them out of your life? Probably the answer to all these is no. You still behaved with love even though you did not feel it at the time. Your heart was still right. In my case, having the person move away from here was truly beneficial for all involved, so my heart's motive was in line. In finding a way to bless them with my words by faith, I got God on the scene. The point is to have the mountain moved, right? I did not have to like them to speak a blessing on them. I just needed to operate in God's love by faith.

Similarly, you do not have to be around someone or speak to them to show God's love. You can hear something about a person and keep it to yourself instead of spreading gossip. You can choose not to treat someone the way your emotions tell you they deserve. This is also love.

God has made it that easy. The right heart motive allowed my faith to work. That mountain was moved within a month. Whatever your situation, ask God for something to speak over it that will show His love. Then do it by faith until it manifests.

No wonder the enemy tries so hard to operate in the feeling realm and cause strife and offenses. It is the one thing that will leave us powerless. Look at these scriptures.

> If I regard iniquity in my heart, The Lord will not hear (Psalm 66:18).

> Beloved, if our heart does not condemn us, we have confidence toward God (I John 3:21).

> For in it, the righteousness of God is revealed
> from **faith** to **faith;** as it is written, "The just shall
> **live by faith"** (Romans 1:17, emphasis mine).

> For in Christ Jesus neither circumcision nor
> uncircumcision avails anything, but faith working
> through love (Galatians 5:6).

> But **without faith** *it is* impossible to please *Him,*
> for he who comes to God must believe that He is,
> and *that* He is a rewarder of those who diligently
> seek Him (Hebrews 11:6, emphasis mine).

God will love others through you in ways you could never think of and could not see yourself doing in the natural. I am wise to this now and often ask God how to think and what to say in a situation that may seem outside the box. I understand now that what He asks is for my spiritual and emotional benefit, even though it may look like it's for the other person only. God designed the process this way. It's like my selfish reasons for forgiving people that I discuss in my first book.[17] If that's how you need to start, then do it; God will work with you.

I have found that it gets easier and easier to bless when I see the results in my life and that feelings have nothing to do with it. It is a secret the enemy does not want you to discover. He will always try to condemn you because your feelings may not match up with your words. He is a liar! Love is not a feeling, it is an action. Sure, feelings are nice, and it would be great to always have good ones, but they are often fleeting and cannot be relied upon. The words you speak and your actions are what you use to operate in biblical faith and love. You can esteem others without feeling like it. You can bless someone with a financial gift without even liking them if God asks you to. You can continue treating your spouse with love and respect even when angry with them. This is the real, mature love that will develop in you as you spend time in God's presence; the real love that will fuel your faith and carry you high above your circumstances. This is the love that wins battles.

CHAPTER 6

A Sound Mind

My son, give attention to my words;
Incline your ear to my sayings. —Proverbs 4:20

SOME MAY FIND THIS PART OF THE TEACHING A LITTLE challenging to wrap themselves around. It carries the concept that you are made in God's image, and, in Him, you can do all things.

The Mind of Christ

> For "who has known the mind of the Lord that
> he may instruct Him?" But we have the mind of
> Christ (I Corinthians 2:16).

That is a strong statement to make and, as such, deserves attention. I looked up the definition of the word "mind" in *Strong's Concordance* ("nous," #3563) and found the definition to say, "knowledge, understanding, intellect, thought or feeling." In other words, we have the ability to think like Jesus. We can know him to the point of understanding His Word, thinking His thoughts, and feeling how He feels. Wow! I am glad God said it; otherwise, I would never believe it.

I was never the sharpest person growing up. I had a lot of negative influences, a poverty mentality, a low self-image, and a minimal amount of secondary education. Even now I know I am not that smart on my own. Many of us are in that boat and we have a hard time accepting that we can have the mind of Christ. Religion will balk at this idea. Some would even cry out, "Blasphemy!" That is just where the enemy would want you. This concept is like all others in God's Word. It has nothing to do with us in our natural ability, but everything to do with Jesus and what He did for us. He is the one who gives us this ability and I am so grateful.

I quickly realized that my only hope for any wisdom or understanding in this life was to immerse myself in God's Word. Man's wisdom or advice would never be able to save me where I was. As with all things in the Bible, if He said it—I believe it. I was desperate for this because I knew how limited I was. I was under no delusion as to my brilliance, as a quick survey of my history reminded me otherwise. That is not a bad thing. I think people of high education and human intelligence may have a more difficult time humbling themselves to God's way of thinking and doing. This was not my issue.

I have found that the more time I spend in God's Word, the smarter I become. I ask God to reveal His wisdom to me and just jump in. I developed boldness, confidence, and decisiveness for no reason other than knowing Him more. I love it.

Before I go any further, I want to go over the definition of the word sound from I Timothy 1:7. It means "discipline, self-control, and bring correction" ("sophronismos," Strong's #4995). Our sound mind comes from the discipline of being in His Word, the self-control to obey what it says, and correcting our thoughts when they are in opposition to His. This may sound heavy, but it surely isn't.

We are required to present our minds, but He is the one who does the work in us. As we spend time with Him, we learn to recognize and hear His voice. When I confess this verse over myself and others, I always add to the last part, "listening to the voice of the Holy Spirit and no other," based on the corresponding teaching in John 10:4 about the good shepherd.[18] A sound mind learns through practice to know the difference between the good shepherd and an imposter, and to act on the right voice speaking. He is the one who gives us the strength to follow through as we spend time in His presence. This is a level playing field. Even if you cannot read, you can listen to the Word being read on audio. If I can tap into the wisdom of God, anyone can.

Work Your Plan

I am a big believer in having an action plan for anything you are trying to change in your life. When I was dealing with depression, I had my scriptures and worship music prepared. I had people who I could go to who knew what I needed. When you are immersing yourself in God's Word to develop the mind of Christ it is no different. Have a plan to keep yourself on track. If you are anything like me, and I suspect it is true, your mind will tend to wander. I have some suggestions for you that worked very well for me.

We are all in the world and being hit with its sights and sounds regularly. Whether it's the job, the grocery store, neighbors, the mall, public gatherings, or simply the TV and radio, we hear and see things we would rather not. Sometimes these things stick in our minds. I am that way with music. It could even be a song I don't like, but I will catch it going through my mind and sometimes I cannot seem to stop it, especially when I am trying to go to sleep. Perhaps you can think of an example or two in your life. It could be an advertising jingle, a shocking image you have seen, or words spoken to you. It can be like a record that keeps playing repeatedly and is so annoying. You don't want it, but there it is. Sometimes there is nothing we can do about these things coming at us but there is something we can do to overcome their effects.

I have a list of recorded worship music that I play and praise along with regularly. I have begun the practice before I go to bed of picking one song that I will sing when the unwanted music starts to go through my mind. You have to do this on purpose, because it's too hard to try and think of a song at the moment. Sometimes it's like the battle of the bands in my head, because the relentless tune will keep coming, interrupted by my worship song. You may have to sing out loud, even as a whisper, so that you can take the thought into captivity. This certainly works, as I have proven, and I eventually fall into a peaceful sleep.

When I struggle with negative thoughts during the day, I can combat them with a scripture verse I have memorized. Pick one for each day and just whisper it to yourself when you need to. As we have learned, the main idea is to just say something else. We answer the negative with a positive. It is easier when I am at home because I can just pull out a good book and start reading. I can put on my worship music or read my Bible. I can pick up a project or hobby that I enjoy and occupy my mind with it.

It is also essential to learn prevention. This can be difficult depending on your circumstances. If you live alone, it is not as hard because you can decide to turn something off. I have a husband who loves certain types of programs and music that acutely bother my spirit. This has been a source of heavy contention in the past and can sometimes still be. I have a very sensitive spirit, and that is not a bad thing, despite anyone else's opinion. Things that get in can take days to get out. When that happens, I am weaker and less able to stand strong.

This happened to me two weeks ago and hit me a bit hard. Something popped up on the TV as soon as I turned it on. I tried to change it, but nothing was working as I am not good with the five remotes it takes to operate a TV system today. By the time I got it off, it was too late; it had gotten in. Throughout the next few days, I was losing my temper quickly, getting upset about things I shouldn't, and blowing it. I had to waste valuable time undoing damage and repenting when I could have avoided it all by pressing the off button quickly.

The enemy is so good at dangling seductive things in front of us disguised as entertainment, education, enlightenment, comic relief, or just plain need to know reality. This trap is as old as Adam and Eve with fruit that seems pleasing to the eyes. Be very selective about what you let in your eye and ear gate. These are the windows to your soul.

I protect my very sensitive spirit fiercely and it causes a measure of fuss. My husband and I have had to come to an agreement that sometimes I just need to walk away. I have to give him a lot of credit here, because he now tries to understand and respect this about me, even though it is foreign to him. He loves the spirit in me and is willing to try and cooperate in what I need, even to the point of just giving up some of the things he likes when with me.

If you are in this situation, I encourage you not to nag, demand, manipulate, or get angry. Do not make it seem you think they are the bad ones. This will not work. You need to try and explain how much it hurts you and reach an acceptable compromise. Remember, you are a speaking spirit and have authority. You can have a major influence in setting the spiritual temperature in your home. Do it God's way and watch Him work.

Improve Your Belief

> Then He touched their eyes, saying, "According to your faith let it be to you" (Matthew 9:29).

> Then Jesus said to the centurion, "Go your way; and as you have believed, *so* let it be done for you" (Matthew 8:13).

Since belief is such an essential part of receiving from God and having our prayers answered, we would benefit greatly from knowing how to study God's Word and know exactly what He is saying. I have heard many people say that scripture is confusing and that there can be many different interpretations. I disagree and I think this attitude can be very dangerous as it will lead people to look for someone to interpret for them—to tell them what God is saying.

There are excellent Bible teachers out there and I am very grateful for them, but I *NEVER* rely on them to the exclusion of studying the Bible for myself. This is the part where a little of that due diligence and being a good soldier comes into play.

> Study to shew thyself approved unto God, a
> workman that needeth not to be ashamed, rightly
> dividing the word of truth (II Timothy 2:15, KJV).

> These were more fair-minded than those in
> Thessalonica, in that they received the word with
> all readiness, and searched the Scriptures daily *to
> find out* whether these things were so (Acts 17:11).

I have found that the best way to know what God is saying is to look up the words in a good Bible concordance. I use *Strong's Exhaustive Concordance of the Bible*. This concordance is easy to use and provides all the original Greek and Hebrew words used to write the Bible at its beginning. As you have read this book (and perhaps my first), I am sure you have noticed how I refer to dictionary definitions to explain a biblical passage more fully. I would venture to say that you cannot diligently study the Bible without doing this, as the Bibles we have are all translations or versions of the original.

Some people say that they only need the Holy Spirit to teach them. If that is you, please refer to the two verses above. Yes, we need the Holy Spirit to bear witness in our spirits as He is the teacher, but we were also told to study. I do not personally know anyone who is so attuned with the Holy Spirit that they understand the entire Bible perfectly. Man will have many opinions to sway us, but the original text is what it is. No one can change the definitions of the words. I will refer back to the word *wrestle* as an example from Ephesians 6:12. In our culture, this word would mean to struggle and fight. In the original language, however, it means "to vibrate fiercely against." This is quite a difference and helps us understand precisely what God is saying.

I will take you step by step in knowing how to use *Strong's Exhaustive Concordance*[19] as a study tool.

Step 1: Determine the word you need to understand. You will find every word used in the Bible in alphabetical order at the beginning of the concordance. They will be arranged in order of appearance, with the corresponding Bible reference.

Step 2: Follow down the list until you come to the verse containing the word you want to look up. There will be a *Strong's* definition number assigned to it.

Step 3: If it is a New Testament word, then look up that number in the Greek dictionary section. You will find the number in the Hebrew dictionary section if it is an Old Testament word.

The definitions are very clear and thorough as a general rule, but sometimes it will tell you the word is a combination of two other words or from a root. When this happens just look up those two number references and combine the definitions or go to the root for clarification and the base meaning. Sometimes it will refer to another number in comparison. Look up those words as well, as they will often give more light and amplify the original word. It is not difficult, and well worth the effort, as it will significantly increase your understanding.

Often, I will take a particularly meaningful verse and write it out from the definitions I find. When I do this, the verse becomes very clear and alive, and I can speak it out in a powerful way in my spirit. The Bible says it is the truth you know that will set you free (John 8:32). I have found this to be true. When I know for sure what something means, then I can have confidence in it; I can believe in it. When I am confident of what God has promised in His Word, I can stand on it. If you are unsure or mistaken, you cannot have confidence. You cannot ask according to His will and receive if you are unsure what He has said.

> Now this is the confidence that we have in Him, that
> if we ask anything according to His will, He hears us.
> And if we know that He hears us, whatever we ask,
> we know that we have the petitions that we have
> asked of Him (I John 5:14-15).

The pivotal statement in these verses is "according to His will." When we know exactly what God has said we can ask for it confidently and know that He hears us. Because we know He hears us, we know we have what we asked for. This is key in learning to fight with the right sword—His sword. I want to give you an assignment concerning this passage as it is so important in your faith life. Please look up the words *ask, hear,* and *know* according to the instructions above, and rewrite this verse for yourself with the expanded definitions. This exercise will make God's Word come alive and be very personal to you. As I have often experienced, He rewards such diligence with more revelation or light. As an added bonus that will bless your socks off look up the word *wealthy* from Psalm 66:12. I would love to hear from you about what you find.

Whenever some of the side effects from cancer and the transplant start to rear their ugly heads, I can confidently lay my hand on that area and declare "peace," because I know what the word means. *Peace* means "Happy, welfare, good health, prosperity, favor, rest, safety, whole, complete" ("shalowm," *Strong's* #7965). Wow, this is one of my favorites. I know all it entails and that is what I expect. I believe God's Word. Claim this as your own.

If I did not know the full meaning of this word God used, then I might not know what I should expect. I have meditated on this word, and I have received God's light on it to the point that when I speak it out, the spiritual vibrations created are effective. Pause and honestly think about this. I believe this practice will help you in any area where you are facing a battle and need a powerful and effective sword.

"Use The Force"

We are all familiar with this phrase from Star Wars. Although fictional, it is a good illustration of what I am saying. God's Word is a powerful force if used correctly. Just like Luke had to practice, concentrate, and understand his tool, so must we. We are "speaking spirits," created in the image of God, and what comes out of our mouths will, without doubt, create our lives. My friends, use God's force for good and not evil. We do not want to give life through our words to what we do not want. I have learned this lesson the hard way so many times that I am confident I am qualified to warn you. The Bible says that out of the abundance of the heart the mouth speaks (Luke 6:45). Please ensure your heart is filled with God's Word so that your mind will direct your heart to your mouth. According to Proverbs 18:21,[20] life and death are in the power of your words, and you will eat the fruit of them. This is sobering.

I am reminded of a lesson I learned from physics that amazed me. We all know that everything is made from atoms. They are the building blocks of all matter. I did not realize until I read a research paper on the subject that the smallest known part within the atom (at the time) was a quark, a sound wave. That tells me that everything began with a sound. It makes sense, doesn't it? Creation began with, "And God said" (Genesis 1:3). Whatever your situation, ensure you answer it with what God says. His words are powerful, and they will be mighty in your life when spoken out of your mouth. Make sure the word seeds planted in your spirit are the good ones that bring you life. If you are in a terrible situation like I was don't worry. If I could get out, so can you. Just start today renewing your mind and prospering your soul.

> Beloved, I pray that you may prosper in all things and be in health, just as your soul prospers (III John 2).

SECTION 3

Stand Still

And Moses said to the people, "Do not be afraid. Stand still, and see the salvation of the LORD, which He will accomplish for you today. For the Egyptians whom you see today, you shall see again no more forever."
—Exodus 14:13

CHAPTER 7

My Position

For you are all sons of God through faith
in Christ Jesus. —Galatians 3:26

AT THE BEGINNING OF THIS BOOK, WE LOOKED AT THE PASSAGE
in II Chronicles 20:17, which tells us, "Position ourselves and
stand still." As good Bible students, of course, we will look up these
words and see precisely what God is telling us to do. We do not find
the word position in the concordance, so we look in the King James
Version to find the original translated word. It is set. This is "yatsab"
and means "to place permanently, to station, to continue to present
yourself, and to stand (fast, still, up)" *(Strong's* #3320). The word
for stand still is "amad" and has almost the same meaning *(Strong's*
#5975). If God told us to position ourselves, then we must have a
position. My favorite passage showing this is Ephesians 2:4-6.

But God, who is rich in mercy, because of His
great love with which He loved us, even when we

> were dead in trespasses, made us alive together
> with Christ (by grace you have been saved), and
> raised *us* up together, and made *us* sit together in
> the heavenly *places* in Christ Jesus.

To understand why we can be in this position we need to go back to the Old Testament and look at the symbolism of coming into covenant with someone. In I Samuel 18:1-4 we see Jonathan and David binding themselves together in covenant by exchanging coats and weapons. The coat symbolized the family authority, and the weapons symbolized the commitment to fight the others' battles. Your enemy is now my enemy, and I will fight.

When Jesus died for us, He cut a covenant with God on our behalf. We now have his robe of righteousness (Isaiah 61:10, II Corinthians 5:21),[21] which means we have standing (a position) in the family of God. There is also an exchange of weapons and a promise to contend for us and back us up. We have all the spiritual armor we need (Ephesians 6:14-18),[22] and when we put it on we are told to stand. The word stand is used three times in this passage. When we are in our position, God will fight the battle.

The Chess Game

I was listening to a minister named Chip Brim a few years ago and he gave an analogy that I thought was brilliant for demonstrating this teaching and giving an understandable picture. He compared walking daily with God to playing a chess game. God will always respond to your move. He is looking for what you are believing, saying, and doing in the situation. When you take your position or make your move based on His Word, He will NEVER fail to make His move. He will always perform and back up His Word.

> Then said the LORD unto me, Thou hast well
> seen: for I will hasten my word to perform it
> (Jeremiah 1:12, KJV).

God is never the problem. His part is easy for Him. He did not break a sweat or wring His hands creating the universe, so He has no issue keeping His Word to us. God will always do in our lives what His Word says when we align ourselves with Him. This is a spiritual law we can count on. We are the ones who get in His way by our fear, worry, anger, and frustration. When we learn to let go of these things and stand confidently in Him, God is quick to deliver. His hand is not short (Isaiah 59:1). I think we all should be walking around like we have a secret. We can "be anxious for nothing" (Philippians 4:6) because we have confidence that God will do what He says.

I am not saying this is easy, because it takes time to train ourselves. Keep practicing, my friends; I have proven this in my life.

No Begging

I learned a very practical lesson about my position last year after I had returned to work full time. While recovering and working part-time, my compensation arrangements changed accordingly, as expected. When I returned to full-time hours, I asked to be reinstated to my original status, which was agreed upon. One cheque came and went with no change, then two, then three. Needless to say, I was getting very frustrated, and my reminders were being ignored. I felt like I was going around in circles, and, in truth, I felt like I was begging.

That was the trigger for me. I was a child of God with authority. I was the head and not the tail, above only and never beneath (Deuteronomy 28:13). What was I doing, begging the world for what I wanted? I knew better than that. I stopped immediately and went to God about it with my scriptures in hand. I asked Him for my raise and position, then set myself at peace and praised and thanked Him for it.

Our faith, words, and "vibrations" are what move things. We accomplish nothing by yelling, nagging, complaining, or begging. That is the world's way, and we are above that. We do not have to fight on their turf. Oh yes, I did get all I asked for a few weeks later.

You may be experiencing an unfair work environment in one way or another. Many of us do. Please take a hard look at how you are responding. Working as unto the Lord (Colossians 3:22-24) is the same lesson as forgiveness; it is for your benefit. When you obey this principle, you have your proper standing before God and have the right to ask for what you need and desire. You can "ask" (demand) for the change according to the scriptural promise you have found and expect all of heaven to back you up.[23]

We are the change conduits on this earth. From the beginning we were commissioned to subdue the earth (Genesis 1:28), take authority (Luke 10:19), speak to the mountains (Mark 11:23), and live surrounded in God's favor (Psalm 5:12). We do not get there by forgetting who we are and resorting to pouting, complaining, manipulation (however slight or unintentional), or reasoning. And please, do not ever get caught in the trap of giving them what they deserve. This will keep the destructive ball rolling and you will play right into the enemy's hands. Be too smart to let him control you.

Let me remind you of your position once again from The Passion Translation:

> But God still loved us with such great love. He is so rich in compassion and mercy. Even when we were dead and doomed in our many sins, he united us into the very life of Christ and saved us by his wonderful grace! He raised us up with Christ the exalted One, and we ascended with him into the glorious perfection and authority of the heavenly realm, for we are now co-seated as one with Christ!
>
> Throughout the coming ages, we will be the visible display of the infinite riches of his grace and kindness, which was showered upon us in Jesus Christ (Ephesians 2:4-7, TPT).

Notice how God mentions the kindness He can show us after He has shown us our position seated with Him. They go together. The book of Psalms contains many references to the outcomes of people who do things from an earthly stance, from their own strength and flesh. It is not pretty. I asked a similar question in my first book: Who has ever gotten results from fighting for their rights, fighting to be heard, trying to control another, crying, silent treatment, accusing, shaming, sarcasm, or throwing tantrums? Show of hands, please. I thought so. These tactics may get grudging compliance for a little bit to shut you down, but it will never last. It never produces real, godly change. Sit in your place with Christ in your heavenly turf and be still in Him.

Psalm 62:5 tells us to wait silently for God alone. I looked up the word wait, and it was very interesting. It is "daman" in Hebrew and means "to hold your peace, to quiet yourself, to be at rest, to stand still and wait" *(Strong's #1826)*. The interesting part is the primary root which means to be dumbstruck in astonishment. The one we are to be astonished by is God. When we see His power, what He has done, and what He has promised us, we are to stand still and at peace in Him alone with complete confidence.

Once again, I will tell on myself as an example. Earlier in my marriage, when I was still growing in these principles, I was undoubtedly fighting with the wrong sword to try and get my husband to change. We had some real issues, and they were very hard on me. I know from experience that the crying, nagging, guilt-tripping, reasoning, and threatening would never produce any lasting change. My concerns were very real and the tears genuine, but none of it was making things any better. It is not because either one of us was a bad person, it is that these strategies are not from God and do not work.

This is the desperate situation I mentioned previously that led to the Holy Spirit prompting me to place anointing oil on my husband's pillow. Along with this, I prayed specific scriptures I had searched out that I wanted to come to pass in our life. I continued to do so, praying that God would speak to him in the night. *Wow, what a brilliant idea,* my lightning-fast mind thought. God does know what He's talking about. I am not saying I have mastered this. I have a temper and some spit and vinegar, but I am learning. I am seeing results.

God is Not Mocked

One thing I want to make very clear to you while you are in the waiting time and it seems like nothing is changing, is that God is never mocked. No one ever gets away with anything and there are always consequences for not listening to God's voice.

I used to struggle with this a lot. I was learning to do things God's way in several areas—being patient, not blowing up, making unselfish compromises, and biting my tongue, only to have the thing I was standing against continue to happen. I do not know how often I sobbed in anguish on the floor because I was hurting so bad and felt like I was being made a fool of. It seemed the other person was just getting away with everything while I suffered silently. Can anyone relate?

This was one of my most challenging lessons because certain things did take a long time. Sometimes there are strongholds that need to be broken down. I had to decide if I trusted God's Word or not. Did I believe He had my back and would answer my prayer? Did I believe that I would have what I continually said in confidence? If you also struggle with this, let me share the verses I stood on.

> For You have maintained my right and my cause;
> You sat on the throne judging in righteousness
> (Psalm 9:4).

> No weapon formed against you shall prosper, and
> every tongue *which* rises against you in judgment
> You shall condemn. This *is* the heritage of the
> servants of the Lord (Isaiah 54:17).

> And the LORD will make you the head and not the
> tail; you shall be above only, and not be beneath,
> if you heed the commandments of the LORD your
> God, which I command you today, and are careful
> to observe them (Deuteronomy 28:13).

Let me remind you that His only command now is to love one another.

> I assure you *and* most solemnly say to you,
> whoever says to this mountain, 'Be lifted up and
> thrown into the sea!' and does not doubt in his
> heart [in God's unlimited power], but believes
> that what he says is going to take place, it will
> be done for him [in accordance with God's will]
> (Mark 11:23, AMP).

I used the Amplified Version here for a reason. When some read at the end, "[in accordance with God's will]," they misunderstand the reference. It is not saying only if God wants it to be moved as that would negate the definitive statement that it will be done. It is saying that this process is God's will for moving mountains. You need to be very specific and have scripture to stand on to truly believe and not doubt. Use the principles taught here to build your faith to the point where those scriptures are solid in your heart.

On a bit of a humorous note, one way you can tell that a mountain is moving is there will be a whole lot of quaking, upheaval, and shaking. It does not want to move and will resist.

Rather than be moved or discouraged by this, rejoice because it is a sign that it is on its way out.

When I learned to settle this in my heart, I stopped looking at things as they appeared. I decided that God was working things out and it was so. Here's a twist. As I began to believe more and more that God had my back and was working on my behalf, I began to be concerned for the other person and what might become of them if they resisted God. I began to know that I was okay and in good hands but the person behaving against me might be in danger.

This realization encouraged me as I was growing past me, me, me! Just a little more growth in loving my neighbor and doing things God's way.

CHAPTER 8

Dealing With Offenses

Catch all the foxes,
   those little foxes,
before they ruin the vineyard of love,
   for the grapevines are blossoming!
—Song of Solomon 2:15 NLT

A S LONG AS WE ARE IN THIS WORLD WE WILL HAVE TO DEAL with offenses, usually daily. They come in every form imaginable, but for the sake of this teaching, I will narrow it down to two viewpoints: how you deal with your own hurt and how you look at the one who hurt you. I find the best way to tackle this is to look at how we view spiritual maturity in ourselves and others.

I have observed and experienced that the problem isn't usually when we know we have aggravated the issue ourselves, said or done something wrong. Most of us recognize when we have been a jerk and caused a fuss; I know I have learned to. The problem usually arises when we know—or think—we are right and have the moral high ground. This is where most of us get into trouble. To begin this, I think we need to look at what real spiritual maturity is and what it looks like.

Real Christian maturity isn't always what you may think. There are a lot of Christians who confuse maturity with religious superiority. I know I have run across a few of these. They are the ones who stand on their soapbox and impatiently correct others or pass judgment on those not deemed at their spiritual level. I know I have been on the receiving end of this type of thing, which is very hurtful. On the surface, one might justify being offended by such behavior. So here is the question to ponder; are you any more mature than they are if you respond to their religious pride with your religious offense? Are we not judging them as well because we think they should know better because of their position in the church or the length of time they have been a Christian? Tough one, isn't it?

No one has too many issues with spiritual babies; we expect them to need cleaning up and allow them time to grow. Where we run into trouble is dealing with the thirty-year-olds still in diapers. Sorry for the nasty visual. You can recognize spiritual maturity in those who show love to people no matter their level or how they may stumble. I had to look at myself because I was offended by these attitudes. It is ok to be disappointed by the behavior of someone from whom you expected better, but not ok to judge them in return or hold anger. We do not know what is going on behind anyone's closed doors and they may be in desperate need of our prayers. Real maturity learns to recognize that anyone can have a wounded soul, no matter their calling or how long they have been a Christian. If that is the first thing that comes to your mind when someone hurts you, then you are well on your way to Christlikeness and true spiritual maturity.

I have had to sit down and honestly count the cost of being "right." Do I ever take the moral high ground, thus automatically judging the person who hurt me as being in the wrong? We may very well be in the right, but how are we treating the situation? We can be right, but with a wrong spirit. This is similar to the scripture, "Be angry and do not sin" (Ephesians 4:26). Anger can just explode, or it can be used as a motivation to correct injustice. One is sin and one is not. It is the same for being right. Are you going to fight for your rights against the other person because you know you are right, or will you use the knowledge that you are on solid biblical ground to position yourself before God for a breakthrough?

I shared in my first book a dire situation where I knew I was in the right. I had to learn the hard way what did not work. I tried all the demanding, fussing, pouting, manipulating, shaming, and crying hysterics, but none worked. No surprise. It will never work for any of us. Being right with the wrong spirit cost me a lot of time, peace, health, and relationship. It is a price I am not willing to pay anymore. God gives us principles in His Word for dealing with offenses that may, at first, leave us feeling, "that's not fair"! God's principles, I have come to experience, are always for our peace and protection. God knows we were not designed to carry anger, unforgiveness, and bitterness. Following His way keeps us peaceful and spiritually healthy and positions us for Him to come into the situation on our behalf and turn it around. I have said this before, only one of you can work in this situation; who do you want it to be, you or God? When we pick it up, God has to put it down.

God the Vindicator

This is another area in which we can separate the girls from the women (or men from the boys), so to speak. The Old Testament is full of stories of the vengeance of God and even David, at times, seemed to have a "Get 'em God" kind of attitude. While it is true that people will reap what they sow and live with the consequences of their actions, it is not our job to wish it upon them or feel justified in it. Being crossways with God is a sobering matter and we do not rejoice in it for any reason. This is not loving, and it displeases God.

> Do not rejoice when your enemy falls, and do not
> let your heart be glad when he stumbles; Lest the
> Lord see it, and it displease Him, And He turn
> away His wrath from him (Proverbs 24:17-18).

One of my greatest lessons was in this area. I have mentioned it previously and will repeat the highlights. God required me to begin to speak blessings over someone who seemed to be ruining my life. I balked at first and told God I did not know how and He would have to show me. The result was somewhat humorous and taught me a great lesson. Praying that they are blessed and prosperous in another part of the country was not wrong as long as my heart's motive was right. God is, after all, on our side as His children. It kind of goes along with loving someone from a distance. This is also not wrong. Some of the thorns in your flesh are a great teaching moment, but do not make the mistake of thinking you have to endure them all forever. God will move them if you go about it His way. God will help you think outside the box and come up with solutions. Within a few months, God handled the situation completely. I believe He would have from the very start if I had positioned myself and done it His way.

When we look at the Old Testament stories, we should do it with the understanding that God is serious about contending with those who contend with you. He does not do it in the same way now, but the consequences are just as serious. God will never be mocked.

> And shall God not avenge His own elect who cry
> out day and night to Him, though He bears long
> with them? I tell you that He will avenge them
> speedily (Luke 18:7-8).

> For You have maintained my right and my cause;
> You sat on the throne judging in righteousness
> (Psalm 9:4).

There is no doubt that God will take care of our situations if we do things His way. It may seem that the wicked are getting away with their behavior, but time and time again in His Word, God assures us they will not. I have learned to pity those who contend with me. They have no idea that they are indeed contending with God and if they do not stop, will suffer for it. I view them as puppets on a string being manipulated by the devil for his purposes. They don't even know what they are doing or why. Remember that we do not wrestle against flesh and blood but against principalities and powers (Ephesians 6:12).

I find that it also helps to remember that this life is so short. People who are crossways with God may enjoy a little pleasure on this earth, but eternity is a long time. We need to have compassion for them. This compassion positions you where God can freely do what He has promised to do on your behalf. Here, we can stand still and see the salvation of our God.

This attitude also applies to your fellow believers. None of us are immune to the consequences of disobedience to God. I know I have felt the natural outcome of my wrong behavior when I did not repent or listen to God. If someone has wronged you, pray for them that God would bring them revelation and repentance. Then speak a blessing over them—whatever you can muster up. Even if it is small, it is a start and will give God something to work with in your situation. Sometimes love can be shown in what you don't say. Sometimes it can be shown in just walking away when there is gossip. Blessing someone does not have to be big or showy, but it will release the power of God in your life.

Taking no notice of a suffered wrong (I Corinthians 13:4-7) is big girl/boy stuff, not for the faint of heart. A very wise teacher once told me this and I have never forgotten it: "What if the first thing God does is reveal to the other person what they are doing wrong?" We do not want to get in His way. You may feel, as I have, that the other person has too stubborn a heart and the situation is hopeless. Isn't it a common attitude that our situation is worse or different from anyone else's? That is why the Bible assures us that our temptations are common to man. He is more than able to solve your issue. His hand is not short.

In Real Life

So, let's bring this all into real life. I think I understand as much as anyone that brokenness happens and is very real and can be debilitating. I have been at the point where I did not care whether I lived or died. I have also been at the moment of fighting the good fight of faith where it would have been easier to die. I have experienced heartache that put stage four cancer on the back burner. This is real life sometimes.

One thing we need to allow ourselves as Christians is the time to process, mourn, or cry at a loss. We are human and have emotions. Some think that to be in faith you are not supposed to feel these things, but that is not so. Even Jesus felt emotions. There is a time for processing and healing, but we do not let it define us forever or steal our lives. I am sure we are all familiar with someone who has never been able to get over a particularly defining moment in their lives. They seem to be a shell of a person or ravaged by bitterness. This is not us. God says in His Word, "Blessed are those who mourn, for they shall be comforted" (Matthew 5:4). This is one of the ministries of the Holy Spirit and He is very good at it. Do not deny your pain, go through it with Him as your helper. Come out to the other side stronger and wiser.

I have spoken previously about having a plan for going through emotional hurt. I will not get into all that here, but I will caution you never to get into self-pity or a stubborn grudge. There is a fine line between healthy crying, purging, and feeling justified or sorry for yourself. We must always focus on and remember what God says about the enemy's intentions. I love it in The Message:

> Don't you see, you planned evil against me, but
> God used those same plans for my good, as you see
> all around you right now (Genesis 50:19-20, MSG).

This is an excellent example in the life of Joseph, but there is also a perfect example in the account of Jesus' crucifixion. Consider the thief next to Him and the amazing outcome. In Luke 23:43, we see Jesus telling this thief that he would be with Him in paradise that very day. What appeared to be the worst day of his life turned out to be the best day. If he had not been there on that cross dying next to Jesus, he would have most likely died in his sin. It was a very unusual and unexpected right place at the right time.

Don't ever despise your situation; instead, look for the opportunity. This could be a defining moment if you allow God into it. My situation was dire but look at me now. Would I have written these books and encouraging blog posts if I had wallowed in self-pity? No! I know it is difficult, but after you have had your initial time processing the sadness or hurt, take a good look at your situation. Don't always focus on what the devil or a person tried to do. Look for a God outcome. Is there a guiding circumstance that will lead you to a stepping stone? Ask God about your response and rest in His peace. After a while, I could take the sword the enemy tried to destroy me with and use it to cut off his head. This is the fun part. Before this happened, though, I needed to recognize what was happening in the spirit realm and take my position in God.

I am always sad when I encounter someone who has not chosen to deal with their offenses God's way. I see them holding onto their grudge and moral high ground, fighting back against someone who has hurt them, sinking more and more each day. I am thinking of one particular person right now who will not let go of their anger and hurt over things said by someone who should have known better. In a conversation one day they commented, "I don't even feel close to God anymore." The problem is they didn't even know why. If you have found yourself in this situation, I can tell you why right now. Refusing to forgive and let things go always only hurts and robs YOU! The enemy will try and convince you of your "rightness," but after a while, because you have the Spirit of God in you, your heart will condemn you. Your spirit will know you are grieving the Holy Spirit. He does not condemn you, but you will do that to yourself. That is when you are on a slippery road to pulling away from God. We were never designed or meant to walk in offense. We do not function well there. If this is you, I beg you, let go of it. Release the hurt to Jesus and let Him get into your situation. Let Him vindicate you and raise you up like He wants to.

I will end this chapter with an illustration to which we can all relate. Have you ever been to the beach and witnessed a lifeguard trying to save someone drowning? If you have watched the ordeal play out, you may have seen the drowning person flailing, panicking, and then clawing and grabbing at the one trying to save them. The lifeguard always tries to get them to stop fighting, calm down, lean on them, and relax, because if they don't, they may also pull him down. I have even heard of instances where the lifeguard had to knock the person out so they both would survive. You know where I'm going, don't you?

When we get blindsided by a problem, like the drowning person, many of us start to panic, flail our hands, fear, worry, and desperately grasp anything we think will help. Oh yes, we pray, but then very often, we just pick it back up and continue on the same course.

Our Heavenly Father is our lifeguard. He says relax, stop fighting for yourself, have faith, and lean on me. God is not surprised; He loves you and has a way out. He will rescue you much better and quicker if you just let go, lean on Him, and do it His way.

CHAPTER 9

Kick the Devil

Wish good for those who harm you; wish them well and do
not curse them. —Romans 12:14 NCV

NOW IT'S TIME FOR THE FUN PART. I HAVE MENTIONED BEFORE
how it gives me a bit of satisfaction to make the devil stomp
away in frustration. I enjoy turning the tables on him. What I am
about to share with you may seem upside down, but isn't that always
the way God does things compared to our natural thought processes?

Wash Their Feet

> "If your enemy is hungry, feed him; If he is thirsty,
> give him a drink; For in so doing you will heap
> coals of fire on his head" (Romans 12:20).

This section was significantly inspired by what I learned watching
the movie *War Room*. In this movie, a married couple is going

through struggles many couples go through as their lives get busy and they start to drift apart. The couple are Christians, but the wife's mother is very much a prayer warrior. In this story, the husband begins to have wandering eyes and puts himself in some very compromising situations. He becomes increasingly dissatisfied with his wife and begins to treat her very critically. When the wife finds out about his indiscretions, she asks her mother for advice. What the mother teaches her is brilliant.

The first thing she asks her is what she wants for her marriage. We have talked about this previously. You need to know what you believe and want in your life. When you have someone to agree with you, you are in more of a power position. There are many things at play in this movie and I would encourage you to watch it, but I will focus on two things here.

The first one will be tough to swallow but you may have already learned this from the re-marriage section of my first book. You may protest, "That's not fair," but hear me through. Remember, no one ever gets away with anything in God's economy. I'm not sure if you have ever given this any thought but if God dealt with David, the man after his own heart, for his sins against Uriah (II Samuel 12:7-12), then how much more do you think He will deal with someone who is hurting you? God is always just and the lifter of our heads. If someone is hurting His beloved, they had better repent.

The mother encourages her daughter to focus on being a blessing to her husband, to treat him as she would a wonderful, faithful husband, because that is what she wants. The Bible refers to this as calling those things that are not as though they were (Romans 4:17). The wife does not want to do it at first, because she feels like we all would, that she would be letting him away with his wrongdoing and she would be playing the fool. The mother finally convinces her to do this in conjunction with prayer and confessing what she wants. She endeavors to only speak about and give life to what she is believing.

The second thing the mother does may seem a little controversial at first glance, but if prayed with the right motive is very scriptural. Knowing that the husband was entertaining the temptation to cheat on his wife, she prays this verse, Proverbs 20:17:

> The food you get by cheating may taste delicious,
> but it turns to gravel (CEV).

> Some men enjoy cheating, but the cake they buy
> with such ill-gotten gain will turn to gravel in
> their mouths (TLB).

I have quoted this in two versions, so you get the picture. They prayed that if he tried to pursue ill-gotten pleasures, he would be physically sick. Here is the part where it may seem a little controversial. You can only pray something like this if your motive is right—if you are doing it to save their soul and for their benefit (see I Corinthians 5:5).[24] This is for serious situations where someone is in danger of a complete shipwreck of their own or another's life. Sure enough, he gets physically sick whenever he tries to meet with that other woman. When he comes home, it is to a loving wife who takes care of him and treats him with kindness.

I do not know if this is based on a true story, but I can imagine how hard this must have been. I can relate to the saying, "faith ain't pretty." As the wife did things God's way, He was able to move on her behalf and change the situation. The husband began to associate cheating with suffering and his wife with joy and love. He repents and their marriage is healed. By washing his feet amid heart-wrenching hurt, while standing in faith, she received her miracle. This principle will work in any situation where you find yourself at odds with someone in your life whether it's a spouse, co-worker, neighbor, or relative. It will spoil the plan of the enemy and give you the victory.

Another form of washing their feet that I have learned to employ is to step outside the hurt feelings and try to see the frame of reference from which someone is behaving. Not everything is as it seems. The gift of empathy and understanding is without measure. Let me give you an example. I was feeling significantly hurt and neglected by someone I had expected to be there for me in a greater way than I was seeing or perceiving. My situation was very serious, and I felt that they didn't care enough. We all have expectations of people in our lives who are close to us and when they seem to disappoint us, it hurts. So I was having my pity party over this and carried it for a long time. It wasn't until I was reading a devotional one day that I looked at it from a whole new perspective.

I knew some things about this person's past and it dawned on me that day that this person thought they were doing a lot for me. They thought they were going above and beyond the call of duty compared to any help they had ever received in their life. What I was seeing as a twenty percent effort was an eighty percent effort in their view. Compared to any help they had ever gotten, they were very much stepping up to the plate. Seeing that was such a revelation, and I could empathize and remove the personal hurt. I washed their feet with understanding and quenched the offense. Always try to look at a problem through the eyes of the other person. In most cases, they are not trying to hurt you and they do care.

Washing the feet of your adversary is also shown in the life of King David. In Psalm 35:12-14 (AMP), we see how he treated the one who was against him.

> They repay me evil for good,
> To the sorrow of my soul
>
> But as for me, when they were sick, my clothing
> was sackcloth (mourning garment);
> I humbled my soul with fasting,
> And I prayed with my head bowed on my chest.
>
> I behaved as if grieving for my friend or
> my brother;
> I bowed down in mourning, as one who sorrows
> for his mother.

Can you imagine how this attitude would make the devil crazy? It is the exact opposite of what he wants and leaves him powerless. Jesus taught this principle as well several times in the New Testament. The most straightforward passage is Matthew 5:44:

> But I say to you, love your enemies, bless those
> who curse you, do good to those who hate you,
> and pray for those who spitefully use you and
> persecute you.

This is what David did and what Jesus Himself did when He was dying on the cross. It may not always change the heart of your adversary because everyone has their own free will but there is a force in the spirit. It will bring freedom to you and set you in a position for God to work in your situation. It will shut down the plan of the enemy to get into your life. If you read further in Psalm 35, you will see that David asked and expected God to vindicate him because of his right attitude. Notice it did not say vengeance. That is God's business. We can expect vindication though, because Isaiah 54:17 says that every voice that rises against you will be shown to be in the wrong (AMPC). Do it through clenched teeth at first if you have to. Remember that faith is a force, not a feeling. The feelings may or may not follow, but do not be moved by that.

I think the most remarkable example of this is Jesus washing the disciples' feet. You need to remember that Judas, his betrayer, was among them. Jesus washed Judas' feet thus displaying for us the full measure of love. It was a very symbolic moment. Following this example is a form of releasing people with a similar force as forgiveness. Jesus was teaching us something compelling here that would bring us freedom.

Count to Ten

Everything the enemy tries to put on you begins with a thought. He has no power over you, so he has to get you to start thinking his way and giving him access. When the enemy comes to try and put thoughts of vengeance, payback, or any doubt or disobedience into your mind, stop and think it through a few steps. Count to ten, so to speak. Ask yourself, "What is he trying to steal from me; what is this going to cost me?" Remember that everything he says is a lie. He cannot speak the truth (John 8:44).25 He will try hard to convince you that something is right but if you give in to him and do it, he will immediately condemn you for doing it. This is the insanity of his methods, and we must be wise to it. We need to catch him at his own game and turn the tables.

I learned this when sharing strategies and principles in my first book. The enemy was relentless in trying to tempt me to break with what I had written, to go crosswise with what God had taught me. He was trying to do this so he could call me a hypocrite. If I gave in to the thoughts and temptations to feel sorry for myself and look at how things seemed, all I wrote would be invalidated. This was his goal. I needed to cast down every one of his bullying suggestions.

His biggest lie was that I would embarrass myself and everyone close to me would be angry. This was not a light suggestion as I did share very personal experiences. I wanted the book to be real and relatable. The enemy practically tortured me with this until I had to scream at him that God would look after me. I had obeyed God and that was enough.

I will share one more personal story that will drive this point home because I want you to see how subtle the enemy can be in this area. None of us are immune without constant diligence. Confession is good for the soul, right? Especially when it is someone else.

A little while ago I got a call to come in right away to see my cancer care team. I was surprised by this as I had been doing very well for so long. I went in, and they expressed concern that my counts had gone up a bit; if that continued, I may have to start treatment again. This did not move me in itself as I know where

I stand and am confident of my expected outcome. The devil did not even try to convince me otherwise, because I was completely at peace. He came at me from a whole other angle, and the truth is, I did not even realize it at first.

Because I know I am called by God to be a writer for Him, I have expressed the desire to be released from my day job so I can do this full-time. It seems like a reasonable desire, doesn't it? Well, the enemy also heard me talking about this and used it against me. He planted the temptation to use this slight rise in counts as a reason to start pursuing long-term benefits so I could be home. After all, I wanted to be about the work God called me to do. I know you are all thinking, Marion, how could you be so blind? This is how subtle the enemy is. He will use God's plan against you if he can. He wanted me to "help" God get me out of work, but the problem was that I would be using the illness I was standing against. This is double mindedness.

I cannot be standing in faith to be delivered from something and then use it for my convenience (James 1:6-8).[26] Sure enough, this course quenched my faith and the counts kept rising. My body was obeying what I was thinking about. We know our imagination is a powerful thing created by God for a reason and we have all seen this in action. I was reading Ephesians 1:18 in The Passion Translation and I found more evidence of this principle. I am using The Passion Translation here because it is the only one that accurately translates the original Greek word considering its roots.

> I pray that the light of God will illuminate the
> eyes of your imagination, flooding you with light,
> until you experience the full revelation of the

> hope of his calling—that is, the wealth of God's
> glorious inheritances that he finds in us, his
> holy ones!

The Passion Translation uses the word *imagination,* whereas other translations use the word *understanding.* I looked this up in *Strong's Concordance* and found that this was correct: "dianoia" (#1271). That particular word is only used a few times in the New Testament and refers to the deep thought of your mind and the channel of its exercise. Imagination equals experience. I always thought it meant spiritual understanding as in other passages, but in this case, it was a completely different word and meaning that changed the whole teaching.

When I went to God about this, He showed me what I was doing and I was dumbfounded. I had not seen it. Of course, I repented immediately and stopped any further steps or thoughts in the direction of long-term benefits. I learned quite a lesson in stopping to count the cost and identifying the origin of any bright idea that pops into my head. I am happy to confess this mistake if it helps you prevent something similar in your life.

Warring for Confidence

I have found that building your confidence in anything you are doing for God takes the diligence and strategy of being in a war. The enemy is relentless in his pursuits to trip you up and keep you in bondage. Don't be intimidated by this though, because you will become stronger and wiser daily. One of the most excellent strategies I have ever found is to keep a journal. This is based on the advice Paul gives Timothy in I Timothy 1:18 to wage a good warfare by the prophecies spoken over him. He wanted him to remember everything God had said and done in his life. It would be reasonable to assume that Timothy had written these things down and reviewed them regularly.

I have found this practice to be of great value in opposing the enemy and his thought darts. When I sense the anointing, I write down everything God says to me. When I look back, I see the consistency of theme and instruction, so I know it is God. I could never come up with it myself. When the enemy comes to tell me I am being foolish and I am not genuinely hearing from God, I have a record of the promptings of the Spirit and evidence that my hearing is sound.

The devil tried this after my first book was finished. The intimidating thoughts came over and over, "Who do you think you are? No one will read your book. Was this really God? You are not a good enough speaker, and you will just make a fool of yourself." This was not a frivolous temptation. On my own, I have little qualification and the enemy knows it. Because I know my limitations, I never sat down to write a word unless I had spent time in the Word of God, prayer, and worship. I knew I needed to be under the anointing for any of this to be worth reading. Because of this practice, and the recording of what He showed me, I can confidently tell the devil to back off.

Another important strategy in warring for confidence is to get over the misconception that love and forgiveness are feelings-based. Both are spiritual forces of our will that will take us far above any abilities of the enemy to convince us of anything. These two forces are about our position, authority, and making a path in our lives for God to move in a big way.

In learning to forgive by faith, I have found that drawing out a domino scenario will help me do the right thing. It's not perfect, but it works. When I am seriously angry (and after I have counted to ten), I sit down and write out what may happen if I react wrongly. How will it affect the relationship and my quality of life if I stay angry? If I push this person out of my life, will it cost me other relationships? Can my body afford to take on this stress? Will the nagging thoughts of this take me away from other things I want to focus on? These are all excellent questions to ask yourself. Most of the time you will conclude that it is just not worth it, and you can decide to forgive by faith for your peace.

While on this subject, I want to address a concern that has been mentioned concerning true forgiveness. People have mistakenly thought that to forgive means you need to be in a restored relationship and exercise trust in that person. May I be so bold as to say that is not true? Although forgiveness is required for your peace of mind and spiritual health, there is no need to keep accepting someone's destructive behavior. Boundaries are necessary sometimes and are not wrong. Only you and God can determine this in your particular situation. I am perfectly at peace with the concept that some people are better loved from a distance. Trust is earned and is wise to remove in some circumstances for your well-being. This is where we need a real revelation that forgiveness is never based on feelings, or you may end up on the side of guilt.

When you do forgive by faith, the spiritual force is immediate, and you can throw it in the devil's face whenever he comes to call. He will want to involve your feelings as that is his turf. You stay on your turf seated with Jesus in heavenly places. This is the place where the enemy cannot reach you and you soar far above. Remember the story of the eagle and the crow? This is the place of confidence that you are His child, you have heard His voice, obeyed, and you can rest in Him.

CONCLUSION

We began this book looking at lessons from the life of David and will end with important examples from the life of Joseph. You cannot help but be impressed by this young man's faith, trust, and patience. Few in scripture were on the receiving end of such unfair treatment without having done anything to provoke it. Some of us relate to David, as we sometimes are the cause of our trouble, but we also need to understand that problems may come even when we have done nothing to deserve it. Trouble is in this world and affects us all. Never forget that the enemy of your soul simply does not like you because of the calling on your life.

Joseph was belittled, ostracized, and scorned by his brothers from childhood, and it culminated with the cruelty of being sold as an enslaved person—all because of jealousy. Although his treatment was unfair and undeserved, we see Joseph displaying nothing but a proper attitude, godly patience, and complete trust in his God. Everywhere he ended up working, he did his best and was faithful, even when continuing to get a raw deal every time. Most of us will know the end of the story from which was coined the phrase, "From the pit to the palace." There was a "one day" for Joseph. The Pharoah of Egypt saw the Spirit of God that was on Joseph and promoted him in one day to be ruler over all the land—right out of prison. The right spirit he displayed through all his trials was his highest qualification for victory and promotion; it is ours as well.

Joseph had received a dream from God long before any of these things happened. Perhaps that is what he held onto all that time as his word from God. Maybe that vision and his belief in it enabled him to keep his heart right through all the trials. There is something to be said for warring by the prophecies spoken (I Timothy 1:18). In my own life, I have had prophecies spoken over me that resonated deep in my spirit. I knew it was God. It has been many years, but I still go over them and speak them over myself because I know they will come to pass. They are a motivating factor for me as well.

I was recently reading the first chapter of James, and, for some reason, it exploded with new understanding for me. I cannot tell you how many times I have read this chapter and never really saw the depth of it. This occurred right after I was blindsided a couple of months before by the unexpected rise in the myeloma cancer counts. What I learned helped me to face this God's way and turn it around for good. I also wrote a sermon called "Persecution or Empowerment?"[27] I saw that perspective is everything.

In James 1:3, the word *power* means "fortitude." When your faith is tested, assuming you passed the test, it builds up fortitude or inner strength. As your strength and fortitude increase, you become more mature and develop stronger character. The culmination in verse four is that at some point you will reach a level of nothing missing, nothing broken. That's what caught my spirit. I saw the trial as a giant maker to reveal who I am inside. The enemy tries to make it a negative, but it is a beautiful opportunity to show what you are made of.

> Through our faith, the mighty power of God
> constantly guards us until our *full* salvation is
> ready to be revealed in the last time. May the
> thought of this cause you to jump for joy, even
> though lately you've had to put up with the grief
> of many trials. But these only reveal the sterling
> core of your faith, which is far more valuable than
> gold that perishes, for even gold is refined by fire.
> *Your authentic faith* will result in even more praise,
> glory, and honor when Jesus the Anointed One is
> revealed (I Peter 1: 5-7, TPT).

You may have heard the phrase that bodybuilders often say: "Pain is just weakness leaving the body." I have a spiritual version of that: "Trials are just unbelief leaving the soul." I often think of Paul and Silas in the lowest dungeon singing praises to God. I wonder if they considered it a trial or just knew something. Paul often spoke of being worthy to suffer for Jesus' name and knew that he was becoming stronger and more victorious with every passed test. A bodybuilder who never wanted any pressure applied to his muscles would cease to be a bodybuilder. They recognize its value. I want to drive the devil mad by having this attitude, by living like I have a secret. If I don't even consider what the devil tries to put over on me as a trial, but as an empowerment opportunity, what is he going to do with that? He will become so frustrated. Bethel does a song that reminds me of this principle. Jen Johnson does a bridge in the song "Way Maker" that goes something like, "I've got joy unspeakable all through the valley … you just can't keep me down!"[28] Sounds like she knows a little about this too.

I know there are lots of people who would disagree with me. I have had people say that I should see it as a trial, because trials are good for you, keeping you humble. It's almost an attitude of respecting the trial. I agree that it is good for you, but my problem with this view is that people often do not try to resist it, leaving the outcome to God and his "mysterious" will. God told us to speak to the mountain. David ran after his trial (giant) with his mouth open. I intend to be that kind of giant slayer.

That reminds me of a funny story. Here I go telling on myself again. During the summer, I was required by my employer to get a COVID-19 test. This was my first time being affected by this situation, and I was a little upset. Because of the cancer treatments, I had some damage to my nostrils and did not want anything put up there. I began to devise ways to get out of it. Do I play the injury card or the anxiety card? As I pondered this, I distinctly heard the Holy Spirit say, "Hey there, giant slayer, after all you've been through, are you going to let a Q-tip take you down?" Needless to say, I sheepishly repented, got a hold of my mind, and went to get the test. God had my back though, as they had another kind of test for people in my situation. I did not need to help Him out with my great idea.

Hardship is often a setup and I have come to believe that with all my being. God loves recompense and harvest. He loves to pour rewards on us when we respond His way, in faith. Can you imagine how pleased God is as your Father when you put your wholehearted trust in Him and go about your life not worrying about a thing? You can imagine it to a point because that's how one would feel when a child treats them that way. Joseph said in Genesis 41:51 that God had made him forget all his former toil. I often say a similar thing based on my knowledge of God as a rewarder: "My future is going to be so good; I won't even remember the past pain." I talk very honestly with God and have said to Him that It will have to be over-the-top amazing to make me forget all this. I believe I will have what I say.

I guess it boils down to confidence in who's got you. Do you know God intimately and trust Him unequivocally? Can you think of someone like this in your life? Someone who always keeps their word and is trustworthy with your secrets and dreams. I hope you can, but even someone like this will let you down occasionally because they are human. God never will though. He is not a man that He should lie (Numbers 23:19). He is the one we need to cling to with all our hearts.

Aren't you so glad that God told the backstories of some of the faith heroes? I am so thankful for His mercies that are new every morning, and that failure in a trial doesn't have to be final. You can repent, turn around, and still turn out well. Abraham was the father of faith, but even he took matters into his own hands at times because of impatience or fear. In Genesis 12, almost immediately after he received God's promise, we see Abraham trying to pass off his wife as his sister because he feared they would be killed. He does it again in Genesis 20. It seems he thought he had to help God keep him alive.

Sarah, Abraham's wife, also felt the need to try and help God with her great idea for solving her hardship. When she saw that she had not yet conceived the promised heir, she decided to give her maid to her husband and obtain a child through her. We are seeing the results of that mistake to this day.

The last one I will mention is Isaac's wife, Rebecca. She wanted to make sure her favorite son received his father's blessing, so she deceived Isaac with a disguise for Jacob. Again, we are seeing this aftermath in the Middle East today.

If these faith heroes could stumble and fall in their belief in God's promise, then we would be wise to keep ourselves in check. Although not to the same extent, I know I have been guilty of trying to squirm out of an uncomfortable trial by taking matters into my own hands. It never turns out well and usually comes with a price to pay. However, I am thankful that this does not disqualify me from being used by God. Like Abraham and Sarah, we can repent and get back on the right road to completely trusting God no matter what it looks like at the moment.

As we come to the end of our time together in this book, I want to leave you with the wonderful confidence given to us in the following verses from Psalms. We certainly can stand still and see the salvation of our God.

> Be still, and know that I *am* God;
> I will be exalted among the nations,
> I will be exalted in the earth!
> (Psalm 46:10).

> So here's what I've learned through it all:
> Leave all your cares and anxieties at the feet of
> the Lord,
> and measureless grace will strengthen you.
> He will watch over his devoted lovers,
> never letting them slip or be overthrown (Psalm
> 55:22-23, TPT).

For they did not gain possession of the land by
    their own sword,
Nor did their own arm save them;
But it was Your right hand, Your arm, and the
    light of Your countenance,
Because You favored them (Psalm 44:3).

With Christ's love,
Marion

PRAYER OF SALVATION

Father in heaven, I believe that you gave your only Son, Jesus, to die for my sins. When I believe in Him, I will not perish but have everlasting life according to John 3:16. I believe in Jesus and accept Him as my personal Lord and Savior. I ask you to forgive my sins. According to your word in John 1:12, I believe that I am now your child, adopted into your family. Thank you, Father. In Jesus' name, Amen.

STUDY GUIDE

For individual or group study

1. Is there something in your life right now that seems like an attack of the enemy, but could be turned around for your good? In what way could God turn the tables on the enemy and bring glory? Could it be in your response? Think outside the box.
   Scripture: Genesis 50:20

   _____

   _____

   _____

2. Find two scriptures that minister to you about God's presence never leaving you and write them below. How do these scriptures make you feel when facing a trial?
   Scripture: Romans 15:13

   _____

   _____

   _____

3. Write down three things you can do as an action plan when you start to feel spiritually dry. Be specific regarding your eye gate, ear gate, and physical action. Make sure it is something you will do.
Scripture: Psalm 150

_____

_____

_____

4. Which one of God's most wonderful, outrageous promises do you have the most trouble accepting for yourself? What could you do to build your faith in this area and improve your belief?
Scripture: Ephesians 3:20

_____

_____

_____

5. Think of a situation in your life that is currently bothering you. Pay attention to what you are saying about it for one week and take notes. After examining what you have been saying can you think of something better that will give life to what you want? Write that down and practice speaking those words.
Scripture: II Corinthians 4:13

_____

_____

_____

6. Write the names of two or three praise and worship songs that you can have on your favorites list at the ready for when you need a recharge. Why do these particular songs minister to you?
   Scripture: Psalm 34:1

_____

_____

_____

7. Which form of worship seems to work best for you when you are facing a difficult decision? Is it praise, being quiet in meditation, or feeding on His Word? Is it a combination? Why do you think this works for you?
   Scripture: Psalm 42:1-2

_____

_____

_____

8. Are there any biblical forms of praise and worship that you are less comfortable with? Why do you think that is? What steps could you take to overcome this to receive the benefits?
   Scripture: II Samuel 6:21-22

_____

_____

_____

9. Think of a time when God moved on your behalf or answered a prayer—no matter how small. Write it below. Use this experience to start a victory journal and continue to write down everything God says to you or does in your life. This is so valuable in overcoming future trials.
   Scripture: I Samuel 17:34-36

   _____

   _____

   _____

10. When you look back at some of the areas of struggle in your life, do you recognize the ground or "turf" that the enemy was standing on? Was it feelings, intimidation, guilt, or pride? What ground were you fighting on? What is the position in Christ from which you should have been responding?
    Scripture: Ephesians 2:4-7

    _____

    _____

    _____

11. Describe some of the things you can do daily to walk in your kingly anointing in Christ. Remember, a king declares.
    Scripture: Revelation 1:5-6

    _____

    _____

    _____

12. Describe some things you can do daily to walk in your priestly anointing before God.

Scripture: I Peter 2:9

_____

_____

_____

_____

13. What is the personality trait you dislike the most about yourself? Brainstorm ways that you imagine God can use such a personality trait. Think outside the box.

Scripture: Psalm 139:13-14

_____

_____

_____

14. Is there a person who has been a significant thorn in your flesh? Is there some small thing you can pray over them to be a blessing that will put you on the right track to a better heart motive?

Scripture: Matthew 5:44

_____

_____

_____

_____

15. What types of outside influences seem to affect you the most? Is it images, sounds, or people's actions? What can you do to be proactive in avoiding these negative influences?
    Scripture: Philippians 4:8

_____

_____

_____

16. Pick one verse that ministers to you in a very real way. Look up all the words in *Strong's Concordance* and rewrite the verse with the expanded definitions. Did you find any additional revelation or light to add to what you already understood about this verse? Was there anything that surprised you?
    Scripture: Acts 17:11

_____

_____

_____

17. What is the difference between faith and feelings? Describe the characteristics of both.
    Scripture: Hebrews 11:1

_____

_____

_____

_____

18. Can you recall a particular situation in which you have tried to fight for your rights or to be heard? Find two scriptures that answer this situation and write them below. For two weeks, respond only by going to God with these scriptures and note the outcome. What happened in your spirit?

Scripture: Psalm 9:4

_____

_____

_____

19. How do you think you could begin to take steps towards taking your thoughts captive? Describe some practical measures you could easily implement daily.

Scripture: Romans 12:2

_____

_____

_____

20. Have you been angry with someone lately and acted upon it? Think about the domino effects and what those actions cost you. How did you feel afterward? What do you think would have been a better response?

Scripture: Psalm 37:6-8

_____

_____

_____

21. What is something you are currently believing God for? Think of a creative way that you can bless someone that would be a seed sown towards your harvest.
    Scripture: Mark 4: 26-28

_____

_____

_____

22. We are told to labor to enter into His rest. What does this look like to you? How can you purposefully and daily practice this?
    Scripture: Hebrews 4: 9-12

_____

_____

_____

REFERENCES

Liedke, Michael D.N.P. (2018) "Neurophysiological Benefits of Worship," *The Journal of Biblical Foundations of Faith and Learning*: Vol. 3: Iss. 1, Article 22. Available at: https://knowledge.e.southern.edu/jbffl/vol3/iss1/22

Leaf, Dr. Caroline. "21-Day Brain Detox Online Course." 21daybraindetox.com.

Madison, Rev. S. "Man is a Speaking Spirit." torahisteaching.com.

Strong, James. *Strong's Exhaustive Concordance of the Bible.* Thomas Nelson Publishers: Nashville, 1990.

Grace, Marion. *Your Greatest Life: Overcoming Depression, Divorce, and Critical Illness.* WestBow Press: Bloomington, IN, 2021.

COMING SOON

Watch for book three in Marion's **Your Greatest Life** series, coming soon:

EVERYTHING TO ME

Living Life in the Outrageous Love of God

Excerpt:

L ET'S FACE IT; LIFE CAN BE JUST PLAIN HARD SOMETIMES. WE face seemingly impossible situations, often one right after the other, and we find ourselves looking up to God and crying out, "Where are you?" At that moment we feel so alone and long for those times when it seemed the sweet breath of God was right in front of our faces. I know, I have been there and it's a tough place to come out of.

When I was in the worst of my battle with cancer and the enemy side swiped me from out of the blue with the worst emotional attack I could ever imagine, I will be honest with you and admit that I spent some time on the floor sobbing to God and gasping for my next breath. I was hurting—badly.

The first thing I want to say about that—because I know you have been there too—is that nothing is wrong with it. You are not weak or faithless. We are human beings with a spirit and a soul. There have been days when my spirit may have been wise and knew what to do but my soul (mind, will, and emotions) was so devastated that I needed the recovery time. I needed the healing and purging effect of tears. If tears were a sign of weakness or lack of faith, why would God save them all in His bottle (Psalm 56:8)? Our loving heavenly Father cares very much about what hurts us and has a plan for restoring our souls.

On the particular occasion mentioned above, when I had done my crying and got my breath back, my spirit kicked in and I got back up. This is the part where I clung to God, moment by moment, and just kept putting one foot in front of the other. This is the season where I dove into His Word to find exactly what I meant to Him. He promises that He will never leave or forsake us and will never take His love from us.

> Keep your lives free from the love of money. Be happy with what you have. God has said, "I will never leave you or let you be alone" (Hebrews 13:5, NLV).

> So now I live with the confidence that there is nothing in the universe with the power to separate us from God's love. I'm convinced that his love will triumph over death, life's troubles, fallen angels, or dark rulers in the heavens. There is nothing in our present or future circumstances that can weaken his love.

There is no power above us or beneath us—
no power that could ever be found in the universe
that can distance us from God's passionate love,
which is lavished upon us through our Lord Jesus,
the Anointed One! (Romans 8: 38-39, TPT).

God respects and will respond to the kind of faith that says, "I know that I mean everything to you. I know you love me more than I can imagine, and you only have good plans for me" (see Jeremiah 29:11). He loves it when we know that about His character. I love the phrase that The Passion Translation uses repeatedly, "His wraparound presence." This speaks of His love being with me always, enveloping me like a blanket.

Friends, there is no one God loves more than you. He knew you before forming you and had a plan for your life. He saves your tears and keeps track of the very hairs on your head. You can confidently say it about Him as much as He says it about you—You are everything to me.

ALSO BY MARION GRACE

YOUR GREATEST LIFE

Overcoming Depression, Divorce, and Critical Illness

This book is the story and journey of a very ordinary Christian woman, one who loves Jesus and believes His word and wants nothing more than to live for Him, a woman who has faith and speaks the word of God over her life.

Like many of you, I was doing all the right things, all the things I had been taught, but was not living in the victory I knew God wanted for me. Many of you, like I was, are wondering, *What is wrong with me? Is there something about me that God is just not happy with? Why do I feel this way?*

This book may not be what you are expecting. It is very raw and honest, and it definitely does not contain churchy or Christianese phrases or canned pat answers. Can anyone be brave enough with me to admit we absolutely cannot stand that?

I believe it contains real answers to very real and all too common problems in the body of Christ today that no one wants to admit or talk about. This is about real life, pressures, tests, decisions, and real consequences. There are hard issues dealt with here, those that will definitely challenge you, but I believe in you. You can handle this.

This book will make you laugh, cry, shout, dance, and maybe scream, but one thing I can tell you is that you will get answers. I have read a hundred self-help books, and the thing that makes this different is more the practical day-to-day how-to. I am a person who wants to know the process, not theory, and I am delivering this to you today. My prayer and desire is to help everyone who reads this book realize how much God loves them and that real victory is not only available to them but close within their reach.

I had my first real encounter with the unconditional love of God when I was deep in the pit of depression and had given up on everything I had been taught to do to live a victorious and prosperous Christian life. I had all the books, and I bet you do too: books like such-and-such steps to financial prosperity, how to keep the devil off your back, how to live in victory, ten things every Christian wife needs to know, and so on. There is a book on how to overcome every imaginable problem we may face. I am not knocking on these books and teachings. I am writing one right now. They are vital to our growth and maturity, and I am thankful for every anointed minister who shares their gifts in this way.

What many of us do not realize, however, is that there is no formula, no matter how good the book is. No one, two, three, and poof you've arrived. There is only an honest and sincere heart of love and obedience before God and standing in and on His Word.

During these times, many years ago I believed I had been doing all of the very sound biblical principles I had been taught, and nothing ever went the way I thought it was supposed to. I was tithing but never getting ahead financially. I was submitting to and respecting my husband, but never feeling like I was receiving the love I expected. I was continually putting the Word in my heart, confessing scripture over things I wanted in my life but never seeing them come to pass.

Years went by like this, and I became more and more discouraged and angry. I did not understand why God would do things for other people and not for me. Of course when you are living as a discouraged and angry person, it tends to spill over into your relationships, especially your marriage. I had become a resentful, cynical, bitter, and offendable person, and as a result, my marriage was falling apart. There was a seed of bitterness toward my husband because, of course, I figured I was doing everything right. So it must be him. Can anyone identify?

This is just where the devil likes to find people. This is where he will start to whisper lies into your ear like, "God does not love you. You will never be good enough. It's that spouse of yours." or "You are a complete failure."

Sure enough, he came along whispering those things to me. I came to the point where I was so disheartened with God and what I thought He was that I literally yelled at Him, "I am not doing this anymore! If I have to jump through all these hoops and do everything perfect to get You to love me or do anything in my life, then I just give up."

And I did. I stopped confessing the Word and studying my Bible. I cut back on church attendance, and I talked to God with very raw honesty and bluntness only when I felt like it.

I have a bit of a spitfire personality, and if I get upset, I can get very spiteful. I grew up on the wrong side of the tracks and had to be a bit of a scrapper to get home from school in one piece a lot of the time. Because this was in me, a bit of that spiteful scrapper came out, and my thought process went a little like this, *I've done everything right, and it's not working. So I'm just going to do everything wrong.* I still loved God but was very disappointed in Him, if you can imagine such a thing.

I had been in a very dark and lonely place for a long time and really did not care if I lived or died. I am being very honest here because I am certain there are those of you who feel or felt that way and would never admit it out loud. You might not even admit it to God.

Let me encourage you with what I discovered through this time of doing everything wrong and being angry, depressed, bitter, and disappointed. The Spirit of God never once for a moment took His presence from me. I guess I expected that He would, but He never did. I remember being in my rebellious, "not giving a rip about anything" moments, and my thoughts would sometimes turn toward God. And a warm feeling would come over me.

This continued on for a couple of years. Every time I would talk to God in my raw, blunt way, even with a glass of wine in my hand, His love would seep into me. My lightning-fast mind finally caught up with my spirit after a while. God did not love me based on how much scripture I confessed or how much I tithed, attended church, prayed, or read my Bible. He just simply loved me. I was doing nothing for Him—and had not for a while—and He still loved me. I felt God's love and presence more during this time than I had ever felt in my entire Christian walk—more than when I had been leading the prayer team and super kid program or teaching in the Bible school.

Does this surprise you? Well, it sure did me. I had always been told, "God cares more about you than about what you do," but I never really knew it until then. Remember in the movie *Avatar* when the female character looks at Sully and says "I see you"? That's how I felt with God at that time. I really saw Him. He is love. I was so excited when I found this in scripture too. Job said the same thing in Job 42:5 (TLB), "I have heard of you but now I see you."

None of us wants to go through the magnitude of trials I did, and I'm not saying we need to. If we do, however, what a reward to receive at the end. It's life-changing. I really believe God would rather have honesty out of our hearts that is not pretty than false flattery for public show. Who do we think we are fooling anyway? He is a big God; He can handle it. God sees your heart, and He can work with honesty.

Looking back now, I realize all that effort in my own strength to please God and trying to get Him to do something for me was the whole problem. It was formulas and religious activity motivated in my benefit rather than a sincere heart of love. God cannot bless human effort, and I cannot earn His favor. He gave me His word to declare over my life as a gift because He loves me, not as a homework assignment to earn a gold star and a reward. I needed to have a revelation of the unconditional love of God just for me because I'm me. In my pit of despair, as ugly as it was, I got it. This period changed my life forever because it changed the way I thought about, loved, looked at, and served God.

I would love to be able to say that was it, that everything was rosy after that, but that was not so. I am very thankful that God did not give up on me during my wacky period and finally got through to me. He knew what I did not: I was about to face the fight of my life. I needed to know how much God loved me in order to survive the life-or-death challenge that came next.

My journey involves three trials that are life-altering in themselves, but more often than not, one will lead to or be affected by the other. Once the enemy gets his foot in the door, he is relentless in his efforts to destroy every area of our lives. This is why we need to be wise to his tactics and resist him before he can gain any territory.

> "Therefore submit to God. Resist the devil and he will flee from you" (James 4:7).

> "Behold, I give you the authority to trample on serpents and scorpions, and over all the power of the enemy, and nothing shall by any means hurt you" (Luke 10:19).

As I mentioned previously, my story starts with depression. That depression led to anger, bitterness, and strife, to the point where it led to a divorce. As many of you are aware, divorce itself can come with its own compounding depression, anger, hurt, guilt, bitterness, unforgiveness, and stress. If you let this go on for a few years unchecked, it can have devastating effects on your physical health. My perfect storm, along with depression and divorce, culminated with a diagnosis of multiple myeloma cancer in the terminal stage.

Because you are reading this book, I am obviously still alive to tell the story. My prayer and desire is to share with you what God has taught me in this storm and to convince you without a shadow of doubt that there is victory for you, no matter how deep in it you are. God is no respecter of persons, and I truly believe that now. The outline of this book will follow my journey as it happened to me. Please read through each section even if you have only experienced one or another of these in your life. Topics will be interwoven, and there will be some repetition as one situation can and often does lead into another and can exist together. (If you are anything like me, it does not hurt to hear it twice.) It doesn't always start with depression. It can start with a divorce, which leads to depression, which can lead to critical illness. It can start with critical illness, which can lead to depression and overwhelming stress, which can lead to divorce.

I know these are heavy and meaty subjects, and I would not even attempt to address them if God had not only taken me through them but brought me out in such inner strength and victory that I could almost count it worth it. (I did say almost.) The devil and I have an understanding. He hates me, and I hate him. Remember that spiteful, scrapper, spitfire part of my personality I described previously? Since he did everything he could to try to destroy me, I have put him on notice that I will do everything I can for the rest of my life to bring deliverance to as many as possible by sharing what God has done for me and taught me. I will make him sorry he ever messed with me.

This is a book of encouragement. The things God taught me are practical and doable for ordinary Christians just like you and me. I just never saw it before. Start at the beginning, one day at a time. If you are reading this, chances are you are already in trouble, so this book will begin with dealing with depression.

> "Beloved, I pray that you may prosper in all things
> and be in health, just as your soul prospers" (3
> John 1:2).

Your soul is your mind, will, and emotions, the target of depression when it comes. When we start to heal in our minds and emotions, it will naturally flow into and bring victory to all areas of life.

> "Being confident of this very thing, that He who
> has begun a good work in you will complete it
> until the day of Jesus Christ" (Philippians 1:6).

My fellow warriors, let's begin.

NOTES

1. "I assure you *and* most solemnly say to you, among those born of women there has not risen *anyone* greater than John the Baptist; yet the one who is least in the kingdom of heaven is greater [in privilege] than he" (Matthew 11:11, AMP).

"I tell you the truth, John the Baptist is greater than any other person ever born, but even the least important person in the kingdom of heaven is greater than John" (Matthew 11:11, NCV).

"I tell you the truth, John the Baptist is greater than any other person ever born, but even the least important person in the kingdom of heaven is greater than John" (Matthew 11:11, PEV).

2. "Never doubt God's mighty power to work in you and accomplish all this. He will achieve infinitely more than your greatest request, your most unbelievable dream, and exceed your wildest imagination! He will outdo them all, for his miraculous power constantly energizes you" (Ephesians 3:20, TPT).

3. "The Holy Spirit raised Jesus from the dead. If the same Holy Spirit lives in you, He will give life to your bodies in the same way" (Romans 8:11, NLV).

4. "Delight yourself also in the Lord, and He will give you the desires *and* secret petitions of your heart" (Psalm 37:4, AMPC).

5. Tradition will teach that this verse is speaking of spiritual healing only. This cannot be so because only the blood of Jesus can deal with the sin issue. The word *stripes* is the Greek word "molops" *(Strong's* #3468): "Blow marks, black eye" and the Hebrew word "chabbuwrah" (#2250): "Beat black and blue, bruise." Bruises did not pay for sin. Isaiah 53:5 uses three words to cover the whole scope of healing, both spiritual and physical. The first word is *wounded*—Hebrew "chalal" (#2490). The root is the same as #2491 with the same meaning, "to slay, pierced to death, killed, deadly wound."

The second word is *bruised*—"daka" (#1792), which means "beat to pieces, crush, destroy, smite." Both of these words are consistent with the teaching that Jesus' death paid the price for our sin. His blood was shed. The bruising black and blue, however, did not involve blood and therefore is referring to another aspect of our healing that Jesus provided. The Greek word for salvation itself, "soteria" (#4991) includes in its definition physical health. The corresponding Hebrew word, "shalowm" (#7965) also includes health. I trust this gives you confidence in God's Word on this matter.

6. "For I know the thoughts that I think toward you, says the LORD, thoughts of peace and not of evil, to give you a future and a hope" (Jeremiah 29:11).

7. My paraphrase of Hebrews 11:1.

8. "But I say to you, love your enemies, bless those who curse you, do good to those who hate you, and pray for those who spitefully use you and persecute you" (Matthew 5:44).

9. "Who delivered us from so great a death, and does deliver us; in whom we trust that He will still deliver us" (II Corinthians 1:10). Our deliverance is past, present, and future.

10. "who also has sealed us and given us the Spirit in our hearts as a guarantee." (II Corinthians 1:22).

11. "For assuredly, I say to you, whoever says to this mountain, 'Be removed and be cast into the sea,' and does not doubt in his heart, but believes that those things he says will be done, he will have whatever he says. [24] Therefore I say to you, whatever things you ask when you pray, believe that you receive *them,* and you will have *them*" (Mark 11:23-24).

12. "I will be in them and you will be in me so that they will be completely one. Then the world will know that you sent me and that you loved them just as much as you loved me" (John 17:23, NCV).

13. "Tread" means "To hit with a single blow, sting, smite, strike" ("pateo," *Strong's* #3961 and #3817, root is "paio"). Our words from God hit the devil hard and quickly and it's done. We cast him like dung.

14. "For the earnest expectation of the creation eagerly waits for the revealing of the sons of God" (Romans 8:19).

15. "And lest I should be exalted above measure by the abundance of the revelations, a thorn in the flesh was given to me, a messenger of Satan to buffet me, lest I be exalted above measure." (II Corinthians 12:7).

16. "Brethren, I write no new commandment to you, but an old commandment which you have had from the beginning. The old commandment is the word which you heard from the beginning. Again, a new commandment I write to you, which thing is true in Him and in you, because the darkness is passing away, and the true light is already shining.

"He who says he is in the light, and hates his brother, is in darkness until now. He who loves his brother abides in the light, and there is no cause for stumbling in him. But he who hates his brother is in darkness and walks in darkness, and does not know where he is going, because the darkness has blinded his eyes" (I John 2:7-11).

17. This is an excerpt from chapter three of my first book, *Your Greatest Life: Overcoming Depression, Divorce, and Critical Illness*

1. Forgiving someone only benefits you, not them. When you choose to forgive someone by faith, not feelings, you are the one who gets peace. It does not matter if the feelings are not there. Forgiveness is a spiritual force (law) that has power in the spiritual realm. The enemy has to respect it. Keep saying by faith, "I forgive," and the feeling may follow in time, but the force is immediate. I had to do this with my father so I know it works.

2. When you choose to hold onto and fester in your unforgiveness toward someone, you are giving them control over your life. For you fellow "control the show" people, I am sure you are not going to allow that. Forgive them and prevent them from having any harmful effect on you. When I realized the truth of this, I let things go because no one is going to control me. No one means that much to me that I will let them destroy my life.

3. Be a thorn in the devil's side. Remember Ephesians 6:12, "For we do not wrestle against flesh and blood but against principalities, against powers." When someone wrongs you, try to remember the source. They are being used by the enemy to come against you. If it helps, think of them on puppet strings being manipulated and feel sorry for them. Forgiving them stops the devil in his tracks and means you are smarter than him. I love this one.

4. Simply, you are more mature and can feel good about yourself.

18. "And when he brings out his own sheep, he goes before them; and the sheep follow him, for they know his voice" (John 10:4).

19. Exhaustive means 100% complete, according to the translation or translations the concordance is indexing. Some concordances are "concise," meaning not all of the words are included. For example, an exhaustive concordance will include every single appearance of articles, prepositions, and conjunctions, like *a, an, the, from, and, but,* etc. Many Bibles will have a concordance in the back, but these have to be very concise to keep the Bible a reasonable size, so they don't bother with the tiny words or all occurrences of every word. This can be helpful, but it is, by nature, limited.

20. "Death and life *are* in the power of the tongue, and those who love it will eat its fruit" (Proverbs 18:21).

21. "I will greatly rejoice in the LORD, My soul shall be joyful in my God; For He has clothed me with the garments of salvation, He has covered me with the robe of

righteousness, As a bridegroom decks *himself* with ornaments, And as a bride adorns *herself* with her jewels (Isaiah 61:10).

"For He made Him who knew no sin *to be* sin for us, that we might become the righteousness of God in Him" (II Corinthians 5:21).

22. "Stand therefore, having girded your waist with truth, having put on the breastplate of righteousness, and having shod your feet with the preparation of the gospel of peace; above all, taking the shield of faith with which you will be able to quench all the fiery darts of the wicked one. And take the helmet of salvation, and the sword of the Spirit, which is the word of God; praying always with all prayer and supplication in the Spirit, being watchful to this end with all perseverance and supplication for all the saints" (Ephesians 6:14-18).

23. This is a very important word to understand as it backs up our position in Christ. Religion will balk at this and possibly say, "blasphemy," but I will prove it from scripture. Look at John 16:23: "And in that day you will ask Me nothing. Most assuredly, I say to you, whatever you ask the Father in My name He will give you."

The first word for *ask* is "erotao," which means, "to pray or entreat" *(Strong's #2065)*. The second word is "aiteo" and means "to call for, require, a demand for something due" (#154). This is also the word used whenever Jesus tells us to ask the Father.

"And in that day you will ask Me nothing. Most assuredly, I say to you, whatever you ask the Father in My name He will give you" (John 14:13).

"And whatever things you ask in prayer, believing, you will receive" (Matthew 21:22).

Jesus purchased this for us with His blood. We have standing with God and can "ask" God for those covenant rights and promises. Please do not stay in bondage with false humility. This is the way God meant for us to live in Him. We have authority on this earth and we have family standing. When we demand what is due in Christ's covenant, we honor Him.

24. "You are to deliver this man over to Satan for physical discipline [to destroy carnal lusts which prompted him to incest], that [his] spirit may [yet] be saved in the day of the Lord Jesus" (I Corinthians 5:5, AMPC).

25. "You are of *your* father the devil, and the desires of your father you want to do. He was a murderer from the beginning, and does not stand in the truth, because there is no truth in him. When he speaks a lie, he speaks from his own *resources,* for he is a liar and the father of it" (John 8:44).

26. "But let him ask in faith, with no doubting, for he who doubts is like a wave of the sea driven and tossed by the wind. For let not that man suppose that he will receive anything from the Lord; he is a double-minded man, unstable in all his ways" (James 1:6-8).

27. Marion Grace Mahar, "Persecution or Empowerment?" Sermon preached at New Covenant Ministries Church, Dartmouth, NS, January 16, 2022. Available at www.mariongrace.ca/events.

28. Bethel Music, "Way Maker – Paul McClure | Moment." YouTube, Sept 23, 2019. Available at https://youtu.be/cHoGEDQQ67o.